THE ESSAYS OF
FRANCIS BACON

Francis Bacon was born in London on January 22, 1561, and died near Highgate on April 9, 1626.

His chief works, English and Latin, include the "Essays" (1597–1625), " The Advancement of Learning " (1605), "Of the Wisdom of the Ancients " (Latin, 1609; English, 1610), " The New Atlantis " (written 1614–18), " Novum Organum " (1620), and " The History of Henry VII." (1622).

The first volume of his Essays, published in 1597, contained only ten. There were several enlarged editions, and the final collection appeared in 1625—fifty-eight essays, including revisions of the original ten. The present edition follows that of 1625, and includes also " Fame " and " The Praise of Knowledge."

"O gentlemen, the time of life is short.
 To spend that shortness basely were too long
 If life did ride upon a dial's point,
 Still ending at the arrival of an hour."

Henry IV. was produced in 1597, and in that same year appeared the first edition of Bacon's *Essays*—a little volume containing only ten numbers, and those for the most part not yet of full proportions. One, however, is concerned with Honour, though not with Honour as known to the poets or heroes of our country. "Honour in its highest sense," says Mr. Atkinson, "was as foreign to Bacon's thought as to his practice. There is not a single word about real Honour in the 1597 Essay. In 1625 a single sentence was devoted to it. Bacon classed it with Ambition and Vain Glory." This is a hard saying, but it can be justified. "A man," says Bacon, "is an ill husband of his *Honour* that entereth into any action, the failing wherein may disgrace him more than the carrying of it through can honour him." And years after he verified his opinion by experience. By that time, though too late, he had added this further discovery to his third edition: "There is an *Honour* likewise, which may be ranked amongst the greatest, which happeneth rarely: that is, of such as sacrifice themselves, to Death or Danger, for the good of their country, as was *M. Regulus,* and the two *Decii.*"

The comparison which has been noted in these two instances of Love and Honour may be pursued further by any one who is interested. But a great deal of the interest will be lost if the inquiry is undertaken in a partisan spirit. There is no good purpose to be served

that great spirits and great business do keep out this
weak passion." Yet we have been told that the greatest
prince of the world, a Roman by a Roman valiantly
vanquished, was an example to the contrary :

> "I am dying, Egypt, dying; only
> I here importune Death awhile, until
> Of many thousand kisses the poor last
> I lay upon thy lips."

The stage was beholding also to Imogen, Rosalind,
Desdemona, Ophelia, Juliet, Perdita . . . and who is
part of the life of man if these are not ? But Bacon
spoke of life as he found it. "I desire to marry (he
wrote to his uncle) with some convenient advancement. . . . I have found out an alderman's daughter,
an handsome maiden, to my liking." This was at
forty-three, and he had six years before begun by being
" in thought to attempt *in genere economico*" the widow
of Sir William Hatton, who was also " well provided."
This was entirely characteristic of the man. " They do
best, who if they cannot but admit *Love*, yet make it
keep quarter, and sever it wholly from their serious
affairs and actions of life: for if it check once with
business, it troubleth men's fortunes, and maketh men
that they can no ways be true to their own ends."
Bacon in this department of business was clearly true
to his own ends ; but as Church said of him, the essay
on Love reveals " an utter incapacity to come near the
subject."

Another acute critic, Mr. A. R. Atkinson, has dealt in
a similar manner with the subject of Honour. It certainly stirred Shakespeare to emotion :

the blame on the necessities of Bacon's life. "He must very early have got into the habit of entertaining thoughts for which persons in authority were not yet ripe, and of looking about for means by which he might alter their judgment. . . . To say this is to say that Bacon must look to achieve a statesman's ends by the means of a courtier, to gain access, to offer services, to watch the rise and fall of favourites. To do so soon became a habit with him, and there is nothing to show that it was ever repulsive to him. The breadth of his intellect left little room for any strength of emotional nature."

The deadly sentence here is that which lays the burden no longer on circumstance, but on original meanness—"there is nothing to show that it was ever repulsive to him." But is the final excuse a valid one? Is it true that breadth of intellect tends to exclude strength of emotional nature? Have other great men never combined the two? or is this combination, on the contrary, a marked characteristic of our most famous poets? At the very moment when Bacon was putting forth his considered views on such subjects as Love, Death, Honour, Friends, was there not one William Shakespeare touching the same regions of human life— not only with the light of an all-penetrating intellect, but also with a sun-like warmth that creates and sustains just and unjust together?

"The stage is more beholding to love, than the life of man," says Bacon. "You may observe, that amongst all the great and worthy persons whereof the memory remaineth, there is not one, that hath been transported to the mad degree of love: which shows mind as body, and it addeth no small reverence to men's manners and actions if they be not altogether open." But he goes his way with an almost incredible naïveté. This particular essay, *Of Simulation and Dissimulation*, is a merciless exposure of his natural attraction towards Machiavellian policy, his inability to practice it successfully, and his insight into the truth of the matter. " A habit of secrecy is both politic and moral . . . the great advantages of simulation and dissimulation are three . . . it is a good shrewd proverb of the Spaniard, *Tell a lie and find a truth* . . . there be also three disadvantages . . . the greatest is that it depriveth a man of one of the most principal instruments of action, which is trust and belief. The best composition and temperature is, to have openness in fame and opinion ; secrecy in habit ; dissimulation in seasonable use ; and a power to feign, if there be no remedy." This is the sum and conclusion of a train of thought which begins three pages back with the words, " Dissimulation is but a faint kind of policy, or wisdom . . . it is the weaker sort of politics that are the great dissemblers." And elsewhere he says, " There is no vice that doth so cover a man with shame, as to be found false and perfidious."

There is a problem here, and the best critics have done what they could to solve it. Dr. Abbot says of the *Essays*: " With all their faults they show Bacon at his best—Bacon as he thought himself to be, and as he wished the world to think of him ; Bacon as he might have been if his better nature had prevailed, and if no temptation had come in his way to bear down his weak intermittent tendencies after good." Gardiner too lays rated by Macaulay in a famous article. Other critics have been more one-sided, eulogizing or condemning to express their own bent and sometimes to serve their own occasions. These advocates have had very little influence upon the jury. By the verdict of generations of his countrymen Bacon was a great man, whose undeniable faults are cancelled by lapse of time and by the intellectual abilities understood to be proved by his Latin works. These are left to experts and antiquaries; only the *Essays* survive, for they are literature, and can never be obsolete. Moreover, they are written in terse and masterly English : the voice of the man can be heard in every line.

As a verdict this will stand ; as a guide to the real interest of the *Essays* it is fatally superficial : it reduces to simplicity, and therefore almost to insignificance, the expression of a character which was extremely complex. And though all men are complex, many divided against themselves, and some as violently so as Bacon, yet the inconsistency is seldom allowed to appear, and very seldom lit up by the searchlight which a great essayist turns upon himself. In Bacon's case the revelation is the more convincing because it is unconscious. He knows he is following Montaigne ; he names him in the essay which he eventually placed first in his own book, and he knows that he is setting down his own thoughts, beliefs, or preferences. But he is no true son of Montaigne : he is not much concerned with feeling ; and if he had been conscious of the revelation of character which he was making on many vital pages, he would probably have given himself " a little scope of dissimulation," for he held decidedly that " nakedness is uncomely, as well in

INTRODUCTION

FRANCIS BACON, youngest son of Sir Nicholas, the Lord Keeper, and nephew of Lord Burleigh, was born in 1561, educated at Trinity College, Cambridge, called to the Bar at Gray's Inn, entered Parliament at the age of twenty-three, and sat there for more than thirty years, during which he was successively Solicitor-General, Attorney-General, and Privy Councillor: finally becoming Lord Keeper and Lord Chancellor, with a peerage, first as Lord Verulam, then as Viscount St. Alban. This appears at a first view to be the typical career of a successful barrister. But there is one striking and unusual detail to be added—in this case the brilliant lawyer and politician was not only the architect, but, as it turned out, the jerry-builder, of his own fortune. He rose by the wisdom of his counsel and the brightness of his intellect, but also by the meanness of his conduct: after helping, as Queen's Counsel, to send his friend Essex to the scaffold, he was convicted as Lord Chancellor of taking money presents from suitors—even from suitors whom he knew he must decide against.

The contrast is too glaring to be missed; it has been summed by Pope in a single witty line, and elabo-

THE ESSAYS
OF FRANCIS BACON

*With an Introduction
by Sir Henry Newbolt*

THOMAS NELSON & SONS LTD
LONDON EDINBURGH PARIS MELBOURNE
TORONTO AND NEW YORK

Nature, he seems never to have pressed the inquiry into the nature and destiny of the human spirit. His *Confession of Faith* contains not one word of personal experience or personal insight. In his *Essays* he shows himself a consummate writer and a great observer of men and of affairs. Yet he degrades human nature as much as he illustrates it, and seasons his dish with mere shrewdness and commonplace as well as with magnanimity and eloquence. Perhaps, after all, this is the secret of his character, his popularity, his immortality : he is not inhumanly perfect, not exemplary, not even further from the ground upon which we ourselves may fall at any time. The inspiring men no doubt are those who are good as well as great ; but they take virtue in their stride so easily and naturally that they seem marked out from the rest of us. It may be consoling, and even useful, to be reminded that the characters of men, and especially perhaps of admirable men, are not always as uniform as they appear, or are made out to be. Men have been great under great difficulties, and their difficulties are inward as often as outward. But we seldom know the truth in such a case, and the rare interest of Bacon's self-revelation in his *Essays* is that here we do know the truth upon irrefutable evidence.

HENRY NEWBOLT.

by ascertaining exactly the degree by which one great man fell short of another: the important point is that he fell short: he was as strikingly deficient in some ways as he was strikingly eminent in others. And since it is true that no man was ever written down except by himself, it must be mainly in his own work that we must look for the proof and the explanation of his deficiency. Perhaps the most revealing inquiry into Bacon's character, unique in its combination of great stature and great weakness, would be effected by reading first his life, and certain of his letters; then his *Essays*, with parts of the Advancement of Learning; and lastly his treatise on Scientific Method, his Moral Philosophy, and his *Confession of Faith*. Before the end, the greatness of his powers and of his achievement will be made clear, and the faults of his conduct will have faded in the mist of time. But from first to last there will be seen the strange deficiency of which we have spoken. He was a great champion of Science; yet the really vast and far-reaching discoveries of his time he ignored or rejected: Harvey, Galileo, Kepler, got no countenance from him. His moral philosophy is based upon two principles, one a natural appetite for good, and for the good of the community rather than of the individual, the other the desire to obey the will of God, in fear of His punishments and in hope of His rewards; but that the first of these principles might be logically independent of the other did not occur to him, nor had he the insight to search for a reconciliation of the two. His piety was genuine but shallow; it was nourished upon words rather than upon thought or feeling— though his great object was to extort all truth from

CONTENTS

CONTENTS

CONTENTS

BACON'S ESSAYS

I

OF TRUTH

"WHAT is truth?" said jesting Pilate, and would not stay for an answer. Certainly there be that delight in giddiness, and count it a bondage to fix a belief—affecting free-will in thinking, as well as in acting—and, though the sects of philosophers of that kind be gone, yet there remain certain discoursing wits which are of the same veins, though there be not so much blood in them as was in those of the ancients. But it is not only the difficulty and labour which men take in finding out of truth; nor again, that, when it is found, it imposeth upon men's thoughts, that doth bring lies in favour; but a natural, though corrupt love of the lie itself. One of the later schools of the Grecians examineth the matter, and is at a stand to think what should be in it, that men should love lies, where neither they make for pleasure, as with poets, nor for advantage, as with the merchant, but for the lie's sake. But I cannot tell : this same truth is a naked and open daylight, that doth not show the masques, and mummeries, and triumphs of the world, half so stately and daintily as candlelights. Truth may perhaps come to the price of a pearl, that showeth best by day ; but it will not rise to the price of a diamond or carbuncle, that showeth best in varied lights. A mixture of a lie doth ever add pleasure. Doth any man doubt, that if there were taken out of men's minds vain opinions, flattering hopes, false valuations, imaginations as one would, and the like, but it would leave the minds of a number of men poor shrunken things, full of melancholy and indisposition, and unpleasing to themselves ? One of the fathers, in great severity, called poesy " vinum dæmonum," because it filleth the imagination, and yet is but with the shadow of a lie. But it is not the lie that passeth through the mind, but the lie that sinketh in and settleth in it that doth the hurt, such as we spake of before. But howsoever these things are thus in men's depraved judgments and affections, yet truth, which only doth judge itself, teacheth that the inquiry of truth, which is the love-making, or wooing of it—the knowledge of truth, which is the presence of it—and the belief of truth, which is the enjoying of it—is the sovereign good of human nature. The first creature of God, in the works of the days, was the light of the sense, the last was the light of reason, and his Sabbath work, ever since, is the illumination of his spirit. First he breathed light upon the face of the matter, or chaos, then he breathed light into the face of man; and still he breatheth and inspireth light into the face of his chosen. The poet, that beautified the sect, that was otherwise inferior to the rest, saith yet excellently well, " It is a pleasure to stand upon the shore, and to see ships tost upon the sea ; a pleasure to stand in the window of a castle, and to see a battle, and the adventures thereof below ; but no pleasure is comparable to the standing upon the vantage ground of truth (a hill not to be commanded, and where the air is always clear and serene), and to see the errors, and wanderings, and mists, and tempests, in the vale below ; " so always that this prospect be with pity, and not with swelling or pride. Certainly it is heaven upon earth to have a man's mind move in charity, rest in providence, and turn upon the poles of truth.

To pass from theological and philosophical truth to the truth of civil business, it will be acknowledged, even by those that practise it

not, that clear and round dealing is the honour
of man's nature, and that mixture of falsehood
is like alloy in coin of gold and silver, which
may make the metal work the better, but it
embaseth it ; for these winding and crooked
courses are the goings of the serpent, which
goeth basely upon the belly, and not upon the
feet.   There is no vice that doth so cover a
man with shame as to be found false and perfidious ; and therefore Montaigne saith prettily,
when he inquired the reason why the word of
the lie should be such a disgrace, and such an
odious charge, " If it be well weighed, to say
that a man lieth, is as much as to say that he
is brave towards God, and a coward towards
man ; for a lie faces God, and shrinks from
man."   Surely the wickedness of falsehood and
breach of faith cannot possibly be so highly
expressed as in that it shall be the last peal to
call the judgments of God upon the generations of men : it being foretold, that when
" Christ cometh," he shall not " find faith
upon earth."

II

OF DEATH

MEN fear death as children fear to go into the dark ; and as that natural fear in children is increased with tales, so is the other. Certainly, the contemplation of death, as the wages of sin, and passage to another world, is holy and religious ; but the fear of it, as a tribute due unto nature, is weak. Yet in religious meditations there is sometimes mixture of vanity and of superstition. You shall read in some of the friars' books of mortification, that a man should think with himself what the pain is, if he have but his finger's end pressed, or tortured, and thereby imagine what the pains of death are when the whole body is corrupted and dissolved ; when many times death passeth with less pain than the torture of a limb—for the most vital parts are not the quickest of sense : and by him that spake only as a philosopher and natural man, it was well said, " Pompa mortis magis terret quam mors

21

ipsa." Groans, and convulsions, and a discoloured face, and friends weeping, and blacks,
and obsequies, and the like, show death terrible.

It is worthy the observing, that there is no
passion in the mind of man so weak, but it
mates and masters the fear of death; and
therefore death is no such terrible enemy when
a man hath so many attendants about him
that can win the combat of him. Revenge
triumphs over death; love slights it; honour
aspireth to it; grief flieth to it; fear pre-
occupateth it; nay, we read, after Otho the
emperor had slain himself, pity (which is the
tenderest of affections) provoked many to die
out of mere compassion to their sovereign, and
as the truest sort of followers. Nay, Seneca
adds, niceness and satiety: "Cogita quamdiu
eadem feceris; mori velle, non tantum fortis,
aut miser, sed etiam fastidiosus potest." "A
man would die, though he were neither valiant
nor miserable, only upon a weariness to do the
same thing so oft over and over." It is no less
worthy to observe, how little alteration in good
spirits the approaches of death make; for they
appear to be the same men till the last instant. Augustus Cæsar died in a compliment:
"Livia, conjugii nostri memor vive, et vale."
Tiberius in dissimulation, as Tacitus saith of
him, "Jam Tiberium vires et corpus, non dis-

simulatio, deserebant : " Vespasian in a jest, sitting upon the stool, " Ut puto Deus fio " : Galba with a sentence, " Feri, si ex re sit populi Romani," holding forth his neck : Septimus Severus in dispatch, " Adeste, si quid mihi restat agendum," and the like. Certainly the Stoics bestowed too much cost upon death, and by their great preparations made it appear more fearful. Better, saith he, " qui finem vitæ extremum inter munera ponat naturæ." It is as natural to die as to be born ; and to a little infant, perhaps, the one is as painful as the other. He that dies in an earnest pursuit is like one that is wounded in hot blood ; who, for the time, scarce feels the hurt ; and therefore a mind fixed and bent upon somewhat that is good doth avert the dolours of death : but, above all, believe it, the sweetest canticle is, " Nunc dimittis," when a man hath obtained worthy ends and expectations. Death hath this also, that it openeth the gate to good fame, and extinguisheth envy : " Extinctus amabitur idem."

III

OF UNITY IN RELIGION

RELIGION being the chief bond of human society, it is a happy thing when itself is well contained within the true bond of unity. The quarrels and divisions about religion were evils unknown to the heathen. The reason was, because the religion of the heathen consisted rather in rites and ceremonies than in any constant belief; for you may imagine what kind of faith theirs was, when the chief doctors and fathers of their church were the poets. But the true God hath this attribute, that He is a jealous God; and therefore his worship and religion will endure no mixture nor partner. We shall therefore speak a few words concerning the unity of the Church; what are the fruits thereof; what the bonds; and what the means.

The fruits of unity (next unto the well-pleasing of God, which is all in all) are two; the one towards those that are without the

Church, the other towards those that are within. For the former, it is certain that heresies and schisms are of all others the greatest scandals, yea, more than corruption of manners ; for as in the natural body a wound or solution of continuity is worse than a corrupt humour, so in the spiritual : so that nothing doth so much keep men out of the Church, and drive men out of the Church, as breach of unity ; and, therefore, whensoever it cometh to that pass that one saith, " Ecce in deserto," another saith, " Ecce in penetralibus,"—that is, when some men seek Christ in the conventicles of heretics, and others in an outward face of a church, that voice had need continually to sound in men's ears, " Nolite exire." The Doctor of the Gentiles (the propriety of whose vocation drew him to have a special care of those without) saith, " If a heathen come in, and hear you speak with several tongues, will he not say that you are mad ? " and, certainly, it is little better : when atheists and profane persons do hear of so many discordant and contrary opinions in religion, it doth avert them from the Church, and maketh them " to sit down in the chair of the scorners."

It is but a light thing to be vouched in so serious a matter, but yet it expresseth well the deformity ; there is a master of scoffing, that in his catalogue of books of a feigned library, sets down this title of a book, *The Morris-Dance of Heretics* : for, indeed, every sect of them hath a diverse posture, or cringe, by themselves, which cannot but move derision in worldlings and depraved politics, who are apt to contemn holy things.

As for the fruit towards those that are within, it is peace, which containeth infinite blessings ; it establisheth faith ; it kindleth charity ; the outward peace of the Church distilleth into peace of conscience, and it turneth the labours of writing and reading controversies into treatises of mortification and devotion.

Concerning the bonds of unity, the true placing of them importeth exceedingly. There appear to be two extremes ; for to certain zealots all speech of pacification is odious. " Is it peace, Jehu ? " " What hast thou to do with peace ? turn thee behind me." Peace is not the matter, but following and party. Contrariwise, certain Laodiceans and lukewarm persons think they may accommodate points of religion by middle ways, and taking part of both, and witty reconcilements, as if they would make an arbitrement between God and man. Both these extremes are to be avoided ; which will be done if the league of Christians, penned by our Saviour Himself, were in the two cross clauses thereof soundly and plainly expounded : " He that is not with us is against us ; " and again, " He that is not against us is with us ; " that is, if the points fundamental, and of substance in religion, were truly discerned and distinguished from points not merely of faith, but of opinion, order, or good intention. This is a thing may seem to many a matter trivial, and done already ; but if it were done less partially, it would be embraced more generally.

Of this I may give only this advice, according to my small model. Men ought to take heed of rending God's Church by two kinds of controversies ; the one is, when the matter of the point controverted is too small and light, nor worth the heat and strife about it, kindled only by contradiction ; for, as it is noted by one of the fathers, Christ's coat indeed had no seam, but the Church's vesture was of divers colours ; whereupon he saith, " In veste varietas sit, scissura non sit,"—they be two things, unity, and uniformity ; the other is, when the matter of the point controverted is great, but it is driven to an over-great subtilty and obscurity, so that it becometh a thing rather ingenious than substantial. A man that is of judgment and understanding shall sometimes hear ignorant men differ, and know well within himself, that those which so differ mean one thing, and yet they themselves would never

agree: and if it come so to pass in that distance
of judgment which is between man and man,
shall we not think that God above, that knows
the heart, doth not discern that frail men, in
some of their contradictions, intend the same
thing and accepteth of both? The nature of
such controversies is excellently expressed by
St. Paul, in the warning and precept that he
giveth concerning the same, " Devita profanas
vocum novitates et oppositiones falsi nominis
scientiæ." Men create oppositions which are
not, and put them into new terms so fixed; as
whereas the meaning ought to govern the term,
the term in effect governeth the meaning.

There be also two false peaces, or unities:
the one, when the peace is grounded but upon
an implicit ignorance; for all colours will agree
in the dark: the other, when it is pieced up
upon a direct admission of contraries in fundamental points; for truth and falsehood in such
things are like the iron and clay in the toes of
Nebuchadnezzar's image—they may cleave but
they will not incorporate.

Concerning the means of procuring unity,
men must beware, that, in the procuring or
muniting of religious unity, they do not dis-
solve and deface the laws of charity and of
human society. There be two swords amongst
Christians, the spiritual and the temporal, and
both have their due office and place in the

maintenance of religion; but we may not take
up the third sword, which is Mahomet's
sword, or like unto it—that is, to propagate
religion by wars, or by sanguinary persecutions to force consciences—except it be in
cases of overt scandal, blasphemy, or inter-
mixture of practice against the state; much
less to nourish seditions; to authorize con-
spiracies and rebellions; to put the sword into
the people's hands, and the like, tending to
the subversion of all government, which is the
ordinance of God; for this is but to dash the
first table against the second; and so to consider men as Christians, as we forget that they
are men. Lucretius the poet, when he beheld
the act of Agamemnon, that could endure the
sacrificing of his own daughter, exclaimed:

" Tantum religio potuit suadere malorum."

What would he have said, if he had known of
the massacre in France, or the powder treason
of England? He would have been seven times
more epicure and atheist than he was: for as
the temporal sword is to be drawn with great
circumspection in cases of religion, so it is a
thing monstrous to put it into the hands of
the common people; let that be left to the
anabaptists and other furies. It was great
blasphemy when the devil said, " I will ascend
and be like the Highest "; but it is greater

blasphemy to personate God, and bring Him
in saying, " I will descend and be like the
prince of darkness " : and what is it better,
to make the cause of religion to descend to
the cruel and execrable actions of murdering
princes, butchery of people, and subversion
of states and governments ? Surely this is to
bring down the Holy Ghost, instead of the
likeness of a dove, in the shape of a vulture or
raven ; and to set out of the bark of a Christian
church, a flag of a bark of pirates and assassins ;
therefore it is most necessary that the Church,
by doctrine and decree, princes by their sword,
and all learning, both Christian and moral, as
by their mercury rod to damn and send to hell
for ever, those facts and opinions tending to
the support of the same, as hath been already
in good part done. Surely in councils concerning religion, that counsel of the apostle
should be prefixed, " Ira hominis non implet
justitiam Dei " ; and it was a notable observation of a wise father, and no less ingenuously
confessed, that those which held and persuaded
pressure of consciences were commonly interested therein themselves for their own ends.

IV

OF REVENGE

REVENGE is a kind of wild justice, which the more Man's nature runs to, the more ought law to weed it out : for as for the first wrong, it does but offend the law ; but the revenge of that wrong putteth the law out of office. Certainly, in taking revenge a man is but even with his enemy, but in passing it over he is superior ; for it is a prince's part to pardon : and Solomon, I am sure, saith, " It is the glory of a man to pass by an offence." That which is past is gone and irrecoverable, and wise men have enough to do with things present and to come ; therefore they do but trifle with themselves, that labour in past matters. There is no man doth a wrong for the wrong's sake, but thereby to purchase himself profit, or pleasure, or honour, or the like ; therefore why should I be angry with a man for loving himself better than me ? And if any man should do wrong, merely out of ill-nature, why, yet it is but like the thorn or brier, which prick and scratch, because they can do no other. The most tolerable sort of revenge is for those wrongs which there is no law to remedy : but then, let a man take heed the revenge be such as there is no law to punish ; else a man's enemy is still beforehand, and it is two for one.

Some, when they take revenge, are desirous the party should know whence it cometh : this is the more generous ; for the delight seemeth to be not so much in doing the hurt, as in making the party repent : but base and crafty cowards are like the arrow that flieth in the dark.

Cosmus, Duke of Florence, had a desperate saying against perfidious or neglecting friends, as if those wrongs were unpardonable. " You shall read," saith he, " that we are commanded to forgive our enemies, but you never read that we are commanded to forgive our friends." But yet the spirit of Job was in a better tune : " Shall we," saith he, " take good at God's hands, and not be content to take evil also ? " and so of friends in a proportion. This is certain, that a man that studieth revenge keeps his own wounds green, which otherwise woul' heal and do well. Public revenges are for the most part fortunate ; as that for the death of Cæsar ; for the death of Pertinax ; for the death of Henry III. of France; and many more. But in private revenges it is not so; nay, rather vindictive persons live the life of witches, who, as they are mischievous, so end they unfortunate.

V

OF ADVERSITY

IT was a high speech of Seneca (after the manner of the Stoics), that the " good things which belong to prosperity are to be wished, but the good things that belong to adversity are to be admired "—" Bona rerum secundarum optabilia, adversarum mirabilia." Certainly, if miracles be the command over nature, they appear most in adversity. It is yet a higher speech of his than the other (much too high for a heathen), " It is true greatness to have in one the frailty of a man, and the security of a God "—" Vere magnum habere fragilitatem hominis, securitatem Dei." This would have done better in poesy, where transcendencies are more allowed ; and the poets, indeed, have been busy with it—for it is in effect the thing which is figured in that strange fiction of the ancient poets, which seemeth not to be without mystery ; nay, and to have some approach to the state of a Christian, " that Hercules, when he went to unbind Prometheus (by whom human nature is represented), sailed the length of the great ocean in an earthen pot or pitcher," lively describing Christian resolution, that saileth in the frail bark of the flesh through the waves of the world. But to speak in a mean, the virtue of prosperity is temperance, the virtue of adversity is fortitude, which in morals is the more heroical virtue. Prosperity is the blessing of the Old Testament, adversity is the blessing of the New, which carrieth the greater benediction, and the clearer revelation of God's favour. Yet even in the Old Testament, if you listen to David's harp, you shall hear as many hearse-like airs as carols ; and the pencil of the Holy Ghost hath laboured more in describing the afflictions of Job than the felicities of Solomon. Prosperity is not without many fears and distastes ; and adversity is not without comforts and hopes. We see in needleworks and embroideries, it is more pleasing to have a lively work upon a sad and solemn ground, than to have a dark and melancholy work upon a lightsome ground : judge, therefore, of the pleasure of the heart by the pleasure of the eye. Certainly virtue is like precious odours, most fragrant where they are incensed, or crushed ; for prosperity doth best discover vice, but adversity doth best discover virtue.

VI

OF SIMULATION AND DIS-
SIMULATION

DISSIMULATION is but a faint kind of policy,
or wisdom—for it asketh a strong wit and a
strong heart to know when to tell truth, and
to do it—therefore it is the weaker sort of
politicians that are the greatest dissemblers.

Tacitus saith, " Livia sorted well with the
arts of her husband, and dissimulation of her
son," attributing arts of policy to Augustus,
and dissimulation to Tiberius; and again,
when Mucianus encourageth Vespasian to take
arms against Vitellius, he saith, " We rise not
against the piercing judgment of Augustus, nor
the extreme caution or closeness of Tiberius."
These properties of arts, or policy, and dissimulation, and closeness, are indeed habits
and faculties several, and to be distinguished;
for if a man have that penetration of judgment
as he can discern what things are to be laid
open, and what to be secreted, and what to be

showed at half-lights, and to whom and when (which indeed are arts of state, and arts of life, as Tacitus well calleth them), to him a habit of dissimulation is a hindrance and a poorness. But if a man cannot obtain to that judgment, then it is left to him generally to be close, and a dissembler; for where a man cannot chuse or vary in particulars, there it is good to take the safest and wariest way in general, like the going softly by one that cannot well see. Certainly the ablest men that ever were, have had all an openness and frankness of dealing, and a name of certainty and veracity; but then they were like horses well managed, for they could tell passing well when to stop or turn, and at such times when they thought the case indeed required dissimulation, if then they used it, it came to pass that the former opinion, spread abroad, of their good faith and clearness of dealing, made them almost invisible.

There be three degrees of this hiding and veiling of a man's self: the first, closeness, reservation, and secrecy,—when a man leaveth himself without observation, or without hold to be taken, what he is; the second, dissimulation in the negative,—when a man lets fall signs and arguments that he is not that he is; and the third, simulation in the affirmative,— when a man industriously and expressly feigns and pretends to be that he is not.

For the first of these, secrecy, it is indeed the virtue of a confessor ; and assuredly the secret man heareth many confessions, for who will open himself to a blab or a babbler ? But if a man be thought secret, it inviteth discovery, as the more close air sucketh in the more open ; and as in confessing, the revealing is not for worldly use, but for the ease of a man's heart ; so secret men come to the knowledge of many things in that kind, while men rather discharge their minds than impart their minds. In few words, mysteries are due to secrecy. Besides (to say truth) nakedness is uncomely, as well in mind as in body ; and it addeth no small reverence to men's manners and actions, if they be not altogether open. As for talkers, and futile persons, they are commonly vain and credulous withal ; for he that talketh what he knoweth will also talk what he knoweth not ; therefore set it down, that a habit of secrecy is both politic and moral ; and in this part it is good that a man's face give his tongue leave to speak ; for the discovery of a man's self, by the tracts of his countenance, is a great weakness and betraying, by how much it is many times more marked and believed than a man's words.

For the second, which is dissimulation, it followeth many times upon secrecy, by a necessity ; so that he that will be secret must be a dissembler in some degree,—for men are too cunning to suffer a man to keep an indifferent carriage between both, and to be secret, without swaying the balance on either side. They will so beset a man with questions, and draw him on, and pick it out of him, that, without an absurd silence, he must show an inclination one way ; or if he do not, they will gather as much by his silence as by his speech. As for equivocations, or oraculous speeches, they cannot hold out long ; so that no man can be secret, except he give himself a little scope of dissimulation, which is, as it were, but the skirts or train of secrecy.

But for the third degree, which is simulation and false profession, that I hold more culpable, and less politic, except it be in great and rare matters ; and, therefore, a general custom of simulation (which is this last degree) is a vice rising either of a natural falseness, or fearfulness, or of a mind that hath some main faults, which, because a man must needs disguise, it maketh him practise simulation in other things, lest his hand should be out of use.

The advantages of simulation and dissimulation are three—first, to lay asleep opposition, and to surprise ; for where a man's intentions are published, it is an alarm to call up all that are against them : the second is, to reserve to a man's self a fair retreat ; for if a man engage himself by a manifest declaration, he must go through, or take a fall : the third is, the better to discover the mind of another ; for to him that opens himself, men will hardly show themselves averse, but will (fair) let him go on, and turn their freedom of speech to freedom of thought ; and therefore it is a good shrewd proverb of the Spaniard, " Tell a lie and find a troth," as if there were no way of discovery but by simulation. There be also three disadvantages to set it even : the first, that simulation and dissimulation commonly carry with them a show of fearfulness, which, in any business, doth spoil the feathers of round flying up to the mark ; the second, that it puzzleth and perplexeth the conceits of many, that perhaps would otherwise co-operate with him, and makes a man walk almost alone to his own ends ; the third, and greatest, is, that it depriveth a man of one of the most principal instruments for action, which is trust and belief. The best composition and temperature is to have openness in fame and opinion ; secrecy in habit ; dissimulation in seasonable use ; and a power to feign, if there be no remedy.

VII

OF PARENTS AND CHILDREN

THE joys of parents are secret, and so are their griefs and fears ; they cannot utter the one, nor they will not utter the other. Children sweeten labours, but they make misfortunes more bitter ; they increase the cares of life, but they mitigate the remembrance of death. The perpetuity by generation is common to beasts ; but memory, merit, and noble works are proper to men—and surely a man shall see the noblest works and foundations have proceeded from childless men, which have sought to express the images of their minds, where those of their bodies have failed—so the care of posterity is most in them that have no posterity. They that are the first raisers of their houses are most indulgent towards their children, beholding them as the continuance, not only of their kind, but of their work ; and so both children and creatures.

The difference in affection of parents to-

wards their several children is many times unequal, and sometimes unworthy, especially in
the mother ; as Solomon saith, " A wise son
rejoiceth the father, but an ungracious son
shames the mother." A man shall see, where
there is a house full of children, one or two
of the eldest respected, and the youngest made
wantons ; but in the midst some that are as it
were forgotten, who, many times, nevertheless,
prove the best. The illiberality of parents, in
allowance towards their children, is a harmful
error, and makes them base, acquaints them
with shifts, makes them sort with mean company, and makes them surfeit more when they
come to plenty ; and therefore the proof is
best when men keep their authority towards
their children, but not their purse. Men have
a foolish manner (both parents, and school-
masters, and servants) in creating and breeding
an emulation between brothers during child-
hood, which many times sorteth to discord
when they are men, and disturbeth families.
The Italians make little difference between
children and nephews, or near kinsfolk ; but
so they be of the lump they care not, though
they pass not through their own body—and, to
say truth, in nature it is much a like matter ;
insomuch that we see a nephew sometimes
resembleth an uncle, or a kinsman, more than
his own parents, as the blood happens. Let

parents choose betimes the vocations and courses they mean their children should take, for then they are most flexible ; and let them not too much apply themselves to the disposition of their children, as thinking they will take best to that which they have most mind to. It is true, that if the affection, or aptness, of the children be extraordinary, then it is good not to cross it ; but generally the precept is good, " Optimum elige, suave et facile illud faciet consuetudo." Younger brothers are commonly fortunate, but seldom or never where the elder are disinherited.

VIII

OF MARRIAGE AND SINGLE LIFE

HE that hath wife and children hath given hostages to fortune; for they are impediments to great enterprises, either of virtue or mischief. Certainly the best works, and of greatest merit for the public, have proceeded from the unmarried or childless men, which, both in affection and means, have married and endowed the public. Yet it were great reason that those that have children should have greatest care of future times, unto which they know they must transmit their dearest pledges. Some there are, who, though they lead a single life, yet their thoughts do end with themselves, and account future times impertinences; nay, there are some other that account wife and children but as bills of charges; nay, more, there are some foolish rich covetous men that take a pride in having no children, because they may be thought so much the richer; for, perhaps, they have heard some talk, " Such a

one is a great rich man," and another except to
it, " Yea, but he hath a great charge of children," as if it were an abatement to his riches.
But the most ordinary cause of a single life is
liberty, especially in certain self-pleasing and
humorous minds, which are so sensible of every
restraint, as they will go near to think their
girdles and garters to be bonds and shackles.
Unmarried men are best friends, best masters,
best servants, but not always best subjects, for
they are light to run away, and almost all
fugitives are of that condition. A single life
doth well with churchmen, for charity will
hardly water the ground where it must first
fill a pool. It is indifferent for judges and
magistrates ; for if they be facile and corrupt,
you shall have a servant five times worse than a
wife. For soldiers, I find the generals commonly, in their hortatives, put men in mind of
their wives and children : and I think the despising of marriage among the Turks maketh
the vulgar soldier more base. Certainly wife
and children are a kind of discipline of
humanity : and single men, though they be
many times more charitable, because their
means are less exhaust, yet, on the other side,
they are more cruel and hard-hearted (good to
make severe inquisitors), because their tender-
ness is not so oft called upon. Grave natures,
led by custom, and therefore constant, are

commonly loving husbands, as was said of Ulysses, "Vetulam suam prætulit immortalitati." Chaste women are often proud and froward, as presuming upon the merit of their chastity. It is one of the best bonds, both of chastity and obedience, in the wife, if she thinks her husband wise, which she will never do if she find him jealous. Wives are young men's mistresses, companions for middle age, and old men's nurses, so as a man may have a quarrel to marry when he will ; but yet he was reputed one of the wise men that made answer to the question when a man should marry—" A young man not yet, an elder man not at all." It is often seen that bad husbands have very good wives ; whether it be that it raiseth the price of their husband's kindness when it comes, or that the wives take a pride in their patience ; but this never fails, if the bad husbands were of their own chusing, against their friends' consent ; for then they will be sure to make good their own folly.

IX

OF ENVY

THERE be none of the affections which have been noted to fascinate or bewitch, but love and envy; they both have vehement wishes, they frame themselves readily into imaginations and suggestions, and they come easily into the eye, especially upon the presence of the objects, which are the points that conduce to fascination, if any such thing there be. We see, likewise, the Scripture calleth envy an evil eye, and the astrologers call the evil influences of the stars evil aspects, so that still there seemeth to be acknowledged, in the act of envy, an ejaculation or irradiation of the eye; nay, some have been so curious as to note, that the times when the stroke or percussion of an envious eye doth most hurt are when the party envied is beheld in glory or triumph, for that sets an edge upon envy; and, besides, at such times, the spirits of the person envied do come forth most into the outward parts, and so meet the blow.

But, leaving these curiosities (though not unworthy to be thought on in fit place), we will handle what persons are apt to envy others ; what persons are most subject to be envied themselves ; and what is the difference between public and private envy.

A man that hath no virtue in himself ever envieth virtue in others—for men's minds will either feed upon their own good, or upon others' evil ; and who wanteth the one will prey upon the other ; and whoso is out of hope to attain another's virtue will seek to come at even hand, by depressing another's fortune.

A man that is busy and inquisitive is commonly envious, for to know much of other men's matters cannot be because all that ado may concern his own estate ; therefore it must needs be that he taketh a kind of play-pleasure in looking upon the fortunes of others ; neither can he that mindeth but his own business find much matter for envy ; for envy is a gadding passion, and walketh the streets, and doth not keep home : " Non est curiosus, quin idem sit malevolus."

Men of noble birth are noted to be envious towards new men when they rise : for the distance is altered ; and it is like a deceit of the eye, that when others come on they think themselves go back.

Deformed persons and eunuchs, and old men and bastards, are envious; for he that cannot possibly mend his own case will do what he can to impair another's; except these defects light upon a very brave and heroical nature, which thinketh to make his natural wants part of his honour; in that it should be said, " That an eunuch, or a lame man, did such great matters; " affecting the honour of a miracle: as it was in Narses the eunuch, and Agesilaus and Tamerlane, that were lame men.

The same is the case of men who rise after calamities and misfortunes; for they are as men fallen out with the times, and think other men's harms a redemption of their own sufferings.

They that desire to excel in too many matters, out of levity and vain-glory, are ever envious, for they cannot want work—it being impossible but many, in some one of those things, should surpass them; which was the character of Adrian the emperor, that mortally envied poets and painters, and artificers in works wherein he had a vein to excel.

Lastly, near kinsfolks and fellows in office, and those that are bred together, are more apt to envy their equals when they are raised; for it doth upbraid unto them their own fortunes, and pointeth at them, and cometh oftener into their remembrance, and incurreth likewise more into the note of others ; and envy ever redoubleth from speech and fame. Cain's envy was the more vile and malignant towards his brother Abel, because, when his sacrifice was better accepted, there was nobody to look on. Thus much for those that are apt to envy.

Concerning those that are more or less subject to envy. First, persons of eminent virtue, when they are advanced, are less envied, for their fortune seemeth but due unto them ; and no man envieth the payment of a debt, but rewards and liberality rather. Again, envy is ever joined with the comparing of a man's self ; and where there is no comparison, no envy—and therefore kings are not envied but by kings. Nevertheless, it is to be noted that unworthy persons are most envied at their first coming in, and afterwards overcome it better ; whereas, contrarywise, persons of worth and merit are most envied when their fortune continueth long ; for by that time, though their virtue be the same, yet it hath not the same lustre, for fresh men grow up to darken it.

Persons of noble blood are less envied in their rising, for it seemeth but right done to their birth : besides, there seemeth not much added to their fortune ; and envy is as the sunbeams, that beat hotter upon a bank, or steep rising ground, than upon a flat ; and, for the same reason, those that are advanced by degrees are less envied than those that are advanced suddenly, and " per saltum."

Those that have joined with their honour great travels, cares, or perils, are less subject to envy ; for men think that they earn their honours hardly, and pity them sometimes, and pity ever healeth envy : wherefore you shall observe, that the more deep and sober sort of politic persons, in their greatness, are ever bemoaning themselves what a life they lead, chanting a " quanta patimur " ; not that they feel it so, but only to abate the edge of envy : but this is to be understood of business that is laid upon men, and not such as they call unto themselves ; for nothing increaseth envy more than an unnecessary and ambitious engrossing of business—and nothing doth extinguish envy more than for a great person to preserve all other inferior officers in their full rights and pre-eminences of their places ; for, by that means, there be so many screens between him and envy.

Above all, those are most subject to envy which carry the greatness of their fortunes in an insolent and proud manner—being never well but while they are showing how great they are, either by outward pomp, or by triumphing over all opposition or competition : whereas wise men will rather do sacrifice to envy, in suffering themselves, sometimes of purpose, to be crossed and overborne in things that do not much concern them. Notwithstanding, so much is true, that the carriage of greatness in a plain and open manner (so it be without arrogancy and vain-glory) doth draw less envy than if it be in a more crafty and cunning fashion ; for in that course a man doth but disavow fortune, and seemeth to be conscious of his own want in worth, and doth but teach others to envy him.

Lastly, to conclude this part, as we said in the beginning that the act of envy had somewhat in it of witchcraft, so there is no other cure of envy but the cure of witchcraft ; and that is, to remove the lot (as they call it), and to lay it upon another ; for which purpose, the wiser sort of great persons bring in ever upon the stage somebody upon whom to derive the envy that would come upon themselves ; sometimes upon ministers and servants, sometimes upon colleagues and associates, and the like ; and, for that turn, there are never wanting some persons of violent and undertaking natures, who, so they may have power and business, will take it at any cost.

Now, to speak of public envy. There is yet some good in public envy, whereas in private there is none ; for public envy is as an ostracism, that eclipseth men when they grow too great ; and therefore it is a bridle also to great ones to keep within bounds.

This envy, being in the Latin word " invidia," goeth in the modern languages by the name of discontentment, of which we shall speak in handling sedition. It is a disease in a State like to infection ; for as infection spreadeth upon that which is sound, and tainteth it, so, when envy is gotten once into a State, it traduceth even the best actions thereof, and turneth them into an ill odour ; and therefore there is little won by intermingling of plausible actions ; for that doth argue but a weakness and fear of envy, which hurteth so much the more ; as it is likewise usual in infections, which, if you fear them, you call them upon you.

This public envy seemeth to bear chiefly upon principal officers or ministers, rather than upon kings and States themselves. But this is a sure rule, that if the envy upon the minister be great, when the cause of it in him is small, or if the envy be general in a manner upon all the ministers of an estate, then the envy (though hidden) is truly upon the State itself. And so much of public envy or discontentment, and the difference thereof from private envy, which was handled in the first place.

We will add this in general, touching the affection of envy, that of all other affections it is the most importune and continual; for of other affections there is occasion given but now and then; and therefore it was well said, "Invidia festos dies non agit," for it is ever working upon some or other. And it is also noted, that love and envy do make a man pine, which other affections do not, because they are not so continual. It is also the vilest affection, and the most depraved; for which cause it is the proper attribute of the Devil, who is called "The envious man, that soweth tares amongst the wheat by night"; as it always cometh to pass, that envy worketh subtilely, and in the dark, and to the prejudice of good things, such as is the wheat.

X

OF LOVE

THE stage is more beholding to love than the life of man ; for as to the stage, love is even matter of comedies, and now and then of tragedies ; but in life it doth much mischief, sometimes like a syren, sometimes like a fury. You may observe, that amongst all the great and worthy persons (whereof the memory remaineth, either ancient or recent) there is not one that hath been transported to the mad degree of love ; which shows that great spirits and great business do keep out this weak passion. You must except, nevertheless, Marcus Antonius, the half-partner of the empire of Rome, and Appius Claudius, the decemvir and lawgiver ; whereof the former was indeed a voluptuous man, and inordinate, but the latter was an austere and wise man : and therefore it seems (though rarely) that love can find entrance, not only into an open heart, but also into a heart well fortified, if watch be

not well kept. It is a poor saying of Epicurus,
" Satis magnum alter alteri theatrum sumus,"
—as if Man, made for the contemplation of
heaven, and all noble objects, should do nothing but kneel before a little idol, and make
himself a subject, though not of the mouth (as
beasts are), yet of the eye, which was given him
for higher purposes.

It is a strange thing to note the excess of
this passion, and how it braves the nature and
value of things by this, that the speaking in a
perpetual hyperbole is comely in nothing but
in love ; neither is it merely in the phrase ;
for whereas it hath been well said, " That the
arch flatterer, with whom all the petty flatterers
have intelligence, is a man's self ; " certainly
the lover is more ; for there was never a proud
man thought so absurdly well of himself as the
lover doth of the person loved ; and therefore
it was well said, " That it is impossible to love
and be wise." Neither doth this weakness
appear to others only, and not to the party
loved, but to the loved most of all, except the
love be reciprocal ; for it is a true rule, that
love is ever rewarded either with the reciprocal,
or with an inward or secret contempt ; by how
much more then men ought to beware of this
passion, which loseth not only other things,
but itself. As for the other losses, the poet's
relation doth well figure them : " That he

that preferred Helena, quitted the gifts of Juno and Pallas;" for whosoever esteemeth too much of amorous affection quitteth both riches and wisdom. This passion hath its floods in the very times of weakness, which are great prosperity and great adversity; though this latter hath been less observed; both which times kindle love, and make it more fervent, and therefore show it to be the child of folly. They do best who, if they cannot but admit love, yet make it keep quarter, and sever it wholly from their serious affairs and actions of life; for if it check once with business, it troubleth men's fortunes, and maketh men that they can no ways be true to their own ends. I know not how, but martial men are given to love: I think it is, but as they are given to wine, for perils commonly ask to be paid in pleasures. There is in man's nature a secret inclination and motion towards love of others, which, if it be not spent upon some one or a few, doth naturally spread itself towards many, and maketh men become humane and charitable, as it is seen sometimes in friars. Nuptial love maketh mankind; friendly love perfecteth it; but wanton love corrupteth and embaseth it.

XI

OF GREAT PLACE

MEN in great place are thrice servants—
servants of the sovereign or State, servants of
fame, and servants of business; so as they have
no freedom, neither in their persons, nor in
their actions, nor in their times. It is a strange
desire to seek power and to lose liberty, or to
seek power over others, and to lose power over
a man's self. The rising unto place is labori-
ous, and by pains men come to greater pains;
and it is sometimes base and by indignities men
come to dignities. The standing is slippery,
and the regress is either a downfall, or at least
an eclipse, which is a melancholy thing:
"Cum non sis qui fueris non esse cur velis
vivere." Nay, men cannot retire when they
would, neither will they when it were reason,
but are impatient of privateness, even in age
and sickness, which require the shadow; like
old townsmen, that will be still sitting at their

street door, though thereby they offer age to
scorn. Certainly great persons had need to
borrow other men's opinions to think themselves happy, for if they judge by their own
feeling, they cannot find it ; but if they think
with themselves what other men think of them,
and that other men would fain be as they are,
then they are happy as it were by report, when,
perhaps, they find the contrary within ; for
they are the first that find their own griefs,
though they be the last that find their own
faults. Certainly, men in great fortunes are
strangers to themselves, and while they are in
the puzzle of business, they have no time to
tend their health, either of body or mind :
" Illi mors gravis incubat, qui notus nimis
omnibus, ignotus moritur sibi." In place there
is licence to do good and evil, whereof the
latter is a curse ; for in evil, the best condition
is not to will, the second not to can. But
power to do good is the true and lawful end
of aspiring ; for good thoughts, though God
accept them, yet towards men are little better
than good dreams, except they be put in act,
and that cannot be without power and place,
as the vantage and commanding ground. Merit
and good works is the end of man's motion,
and conscience of the same is the accomplish-
ment of man's rest ; for if a man can be partaker of God's theatre, he shall likewise be

partaker of God's rest: " Et conversus Deus,
ut aspiceret opera, quae fecerunt manus suae,
vidit quod omnia essent bona nimis"; and
then the Sabbath. In the discharge of thy
place set before thee the best examples, for
imitation is a globe of precepts; and after a
time set before thee thine own example, and
examine thyself strictly whether thou didst not
best at first. Neglect not also the examples of
those that have carried themselves ill in the
same place; not to set off thyself by taxing
their memory, but to direct thyself what to
avoid. Reform, therefore, without bravery or
scandal of former times and persons; but yet
set it down to thyself, as well to create good
precedents as to follow them. Reduce things
to the first institution, and observe wherein
and how they have degenerated; but yet ask
counsel of both times—of the ancient time
what is best, and of the later time what is fittest.
Seek to make thy course regular, that men may
know beforehand what they may expect; but
be not too positive and peremptory, and express thyself well when thou digressest from
thy rule. Preserve the right of thy place, but
stir not questions of jurisdiction; and rather
assume thy right in silence, and *de facto*, than
voice it with claims and challenges. Preserve
likewise the rights of inferior places, and think
it more honour to direct in chief than to be

busy in all. Embrace and invite helps and advices touching the execution of thy place; and do not drive away such as bring thee information, as meddlers, but accept of them in good part.

The vices of authority are chiefly four: delays, corruption, roughness, and facility. For delays, give easy access; keep times appointed; go through with that which is in hand, and interlace not business but of necessity. For corruption, do not only bind thine own hands or thy servants' hands from taking, but bind the hands of suitors also from offering; for integrity used doth the one, but integrity professed, and with a manifest detestation of bribery, doth the other; and avoid not only the fault, but the suspicion. Whosoever is found variable, and changeth manifestly without manifest cause, giveth suspicion of corruption; therefore, always, when thou changest thine opinion or course, profess it plainly, and declare it, together with the reasons that move thee to change, and do not think to steal it. A servant or a favourite, if he be inward, and no other apparent cause of esteem, is commonly thought but a by-way to close corruption. For roughness, it is a needless cause of discontent: severity breedeth fear, but roughness breedeth hate. Even reproofs from authority ought to be grave, and not

taunting. As for facility, it is worse than
bribery, for bribes come but now and then ;
but if importunity or idle respects lead a
man, he shall never be without ; as Solomon
saith, " To respect persons it is not good, for
such a man will transgress for a piece of
bread."

It is most true what was anciently spoken—
" A place showeth the man ; and it showeth
some to the better, and some to the worse."
" Omnium consensu, capax imperii, nisi im-
perasset," saith Tacitus of Galba ; but of
Vespasian he saith, " Solus imperantium, Vespasianus mutatus in melius "—though the one
was meant of sufficiency, the other of manners
and affection. It is an assured sign of a worthy
and generous spirit, whom honour amends—
for honour is, or should be, the place of virtue
—and as in nature things move violently to
their place, and calmly in their place, so virtue
in ambition is violent, in authority settled and
calm. All rising to great place is by a winding
stair ; and if there be factions, it is good to
side a man's self whilst he is in the rising, and
to balance himself when he is placed. Use the
memory of thy predecessor fairly and tenderly ;
for if thou dost not, it is a debt will surely be
paid when thou art gone. If thou have colleagues, respect them ; and rather call them
when they look not for it, than exclude them

when they have reason to look to be called. Be not too sensible or too remembering of thy place in conversation and private answers to suitors ; but let it rather be said, " When he sits in place, he is another man."

XII

OF BOLDNESS

IT is a trivial grammar-school text, but yet worthy a wise man's consideration : question was asked of Demosthenes, what was the chief part of an orator ? He answered, action : what next ? action : what next again ? action. He said it that knew it best, and had by nature himself no advantage in that he commended. A strange thing, that that part of an orator which is but superficial, and rather the virtue of a player, should be placed so high above those other noble parts, of invention, elocution, and the rest ; nay, almost alone, as if it were all in all. But the reason is plain. There is in human nature generally more of the fool than of the wise ; and therefore those faculties by which the foolish part of men's minds is taken are most potent. Wonderful like is the case of boldness in civil business ; what first ? boldness : what second and third ? boldness. And yet boldness is a child of ignorance and baseness, far inferior to other parts : but, nevertheless, it doth fascinate, and bind hand and foot those that are either shallow in judgment or weak in courage, which are the greatest part, yea, and prevaileth with wise men at weak times ; therefore we see it hath done wonders in popular States, but with senates and princes less—and more, ever upon the first entrance of bold persons into action, than soon after ; for boldness is an ill keeper of promise. Surely, as there are mountebanks for the natural body, so there are mountebanks for the politic Body —men that undertake great cures, and perhaps have been lucky in two or three experiments, but want the grounds of science, and therefore cannot hold out. Nay, you shall see a bold fellow many times do Mahomet's miracle. Mahomet made the people believe that he could call a hill to him, and from the top of it offer up his prayers for the observers of his law. The people assembled ; Mahomet called the hill to come to him again and again ; and when the hill stood still, he was never a whit abashed, but said, " If the hill will not come to Mahomet, Mahomet will go to the hill." So these men, when they have promised great matters, and failed most shamefully, yet, if they have the perfection of boldness, they will but slight it over, and make a turn, and no more ado. Certainly, to men of great judg-

3

ment, bold persons are sport to behold—nay, and to the vulgar also boldness hath somewhat of the ridiculous : for, if absurdity be the subject of laughter, doubt you not but great boldness is seldom without some absurdity : especially it is a sport to see when a bold fellow is out of countenance, for that puts his face into a most shrunken and wooden posture, as needs it must—for in bashfulness the spirits do a little go and come—but with bold men, upon like occasion, they stand at a stay ; like a stale at chess, where it is no mate, but yet the game cannot stir ; but this last were fitter for a satire than for a serious observation. This is well to be weighed, that boldness is ever blind, for it seeth not dangers and inconveniences : therefore it is ill in counsel, good in execution ; so that the right use of bold persons is, that they never command in chief, but be seconds, and under the direction of others ; for in counsel it is good to see dangers, and in execution not to see them, except they be very great.

BACON'S ESSAYS

XIII

OF GOODNESS, AND GOODNESS OF NATURE

I TAKE goodness in this sense,—the affecting of the weal of men, which is that the Grecians call Philanthropia ; and the word humanity, as it is used, is a little too light to express it. Goodness, I call the habit, and goodness of nature the inclination. This, of all virtues and dignities of the mind, is the greatest, being the character of the Deity ; and without it, man is a busy, mischievous, wretched thing, no better than a kind of vermin. Goodness answers to the theological virtue, Charity, and admits no excess but error. The desire of power in excess caused the angels to fall—the desire of knowledge in excess caused Man to fall ; but in charity there is no excess, neither can angel or Man come in danger by it. The inclination to goodness is imprinted deeply in the nature of Man ; insomuch, that if it issue not towards men, it will take unto other living creatures ;

as it is seen in the Turks, a cruel people, who, nevertheless, are kind to beasts, give alms to dogs and birds, insomuch as Busbechius reporteth, a Christian boy in Constantinople had liked to have been stoned for gagging, in a waggishness, a long-billed fowl. Errors, indeed, in this virtue, in goodness or charity, may be committed. The Italians have of it an ungracious proverb, "Tanto buon che val niente," and one of the doctors of Italy, Nicholas Machiavel, had the confidence to put in writing, almost in plain terms, "That the Christian faith had given up good men in prey to those who are tyrannical and unjust:" which he spake, because, indeed, there was never law, or sect, or opinion, did so much magnify goodness as the Christian religion doth; therefore, to avoid the scandal, and the danger both, it is good to take knowledge of the errors of a habit so excellent. Seek the good of other men, but be not in bondage to their faces or fancies; for that is but facility or softness, which taketh an honest mind prisoner. Neither give thou Æsop's cock a gem, who would be better pleased and happier if he had a barley-corn. The example of God teacheth the lesson truly: "He sendeth his rain, and maketh his sun to shine upon the just and the unjust;" but he doth not rain wealth nor shine honour and virtues upon men equally: common benefits are to be communicated with all, but peculiar benefits with choice. And beware how in making the portraiture thou breakest the pattern; for divinity maketh the love of ourselves the pattern—the love of our neighbours but the portraiture: " Sell all thou hast, and give it to the poor, and follow me ; " but sell not all thou hast, except thou come and follow me—that is, except thou have a vocation wherein thou mayest do as much good with little means as with great—for otherwise, in feeding the streams thou driest the fountain.

Neither is there only a habit of goodness directed by right reason ; but there is in some men, even in nature, a disposition towards it, as, on the other side, there is a natural malignity ; for there be that in their nature do not affect the good of others. The lighter sort of malignity turneth but to a crossness, or frowardness, or aptness to oppose, or difficileness, or the like ; but the deeper sort to envy and mere mischief. Such men, in other men's calamities, are, as it were, in season, and are ever on the loading part—not so good as the dogs that licked Lazarus' sores, but like flies that are still buzzing upon anything that is raw—misanthropi [men haters], that make it their practice to bring men to the bough, and yet never have a tree for the purpose in their gardens, as Timon had : such dispositions are the very errors of human nature, and they are the fittest timber to make great politics of—like to knee-timber, that is good for ships that are ordained to be tossed, but not for building houses that shall stand firm.

The parts and signs of goodness are many. If a man be gracious and courteous to strangers, it shows he is a citizen of the world, and that his heart is no island cut off from other lands, but a continent that joins to them,—if he be compassionate towards the afflictions of others, it shows that his heart is like the noble tree that is wounded itself when it gives the balm, —if he easily pardons and remits offences, it shows that his mind is planted above injuries, so that he cannot be shot,—if he be thankful for small benefits, it shows that he weighs men's minds, and not their trash ; but, above all, if he have St. Paul's perfection, that he would wish to be an anathema from Christ, for the salvation of his brethren, it shows much of a divine nature, and a kind of conformity with Christ himself.

XIV

OF NOBILITY

WE will speak of nobility first as a portion of
an estate, then as a condition of particular persons. A monarchy where there is no nobility
at all is ever a pure and absolute tyranny,
as that of the Turks ; for nobility attempers
sovereignty, and draws the eyes of the people
somewhat aside from the line royal : but for
democracies, they need it not, and they are
commonly more quiet, and less subject to
sedition than where there are stirps of nobles
—for men's eyes are upon the business, and
not upon the persons ; or, if upon the persons,
it is for the business' sake, as fittest, and not
for flags and pedigree. We see the Switzers
last well, notwithstanding their diversity of religion and of cantons ; for utility is their bond,
and not respects. The United Provinces of
the Low Countries in their government excel ;
for where there is an equality, the consulta-
tions are more indifferent, and the payments

and tributes more cheerful. A great and
potent nobility addeth majesty to a monarch,
but diminisheth power ; and putteth life
and spirit into the people, but presseth their
fortune. It is well when nobles are not too
great for sovereignty, nor for justice ; and yet
maintained in that height, as the insolency
of inferiors may be broken upon them before
it come on too fast upon the majesty of kings.
A numerous nobility causeth poverty and inconvenience in a State, for it is a surcharge of
expense ; and besides, it being of necessity
that many of the nobility fall in time to be
weak in fortune, it maketh a kind of disproportion between honour and means.

As for nobility in particular persons, it is
a reverend thing to see an ancient castle or
building not in decay, or to see a fair timber
tree sound and perfect ; how much more to
behold an ancient noble family, which hath
stood against the waves and weathers of time !
—for new nobility is but the act of power,
but ancient nobility is the act of time. Those
that are first raised to nobility are commonly
more virtuous, but less innocent, than their
descendants—for there is rarely any rising but
by a commixture of good and evil arts,—but it
is reason the memory of their virtues remain to
their posterity, and their faults die with themselves. Nobility of birth commonly abateth

industry; and he that is not industrious envieth him that is: besides, noble persons cannot go much higher; and he that standeth at a stay when others rise can hardly avoid motions of envy. On the other side, nobility extinguisheth the passive envy from others towards them, because they are in possession of honour. Certainly, kings that have able men of their nobility shall find ease in employing them, and a better slide into their business; for people naturally bend to them as born in some sort to command.

XV

OF SEDITIONS AND TROUBLES

SHEPHERDS of people had need know the calendars of tempests of State, which are commonly greatest when things grow to equality, as natural tempests about the equinoctia ; and as there are certain hollow blasts of wind and secret swellings of seas before a tempest, so are there in States :—

> ——" Ille etiam cæcos instare tumultus
> Sæpe monet, fraudesque et operta tumes cere bella."

Libels and licentious discourses against the State, when they are frequent and open ; and in like sort, false news often running up and down to the disadvantage of the State, and hastily embraced, are amongst the signs of troubles. Virgil, giving the pedigree of fame, saith, she was sister to the giants :—

> " Illam terra parens, ira irritata deorum,
> Extremam (ut perhibent) Cœo Enceladoque sororem
> Progenuit."

As if fames were the relics of seditions past ;
but they are no less indeed the preludes of
seditions to come. Howsoever, he noted it
right, that seditious tumults and seditious
fames differ no more but as brother and sister,
masculine and feminine—especially if it come
to that, that the best actions of a State, and
the most plausible, and which ought to give
greatest contentment, are taken in ill sense,
and traduced ; for that shows the envy great,
as Tacitus saith, " Conflata magna invidia, seu
bene, seu male, gesta premunt." Neither doth
it follow, that because these fames are a sign of
troubles, that the suppressing of them with too
much severity should be a remedy of troubles ;
for the despising of them many times checks
them best, and the going about to stop them
doth but make a wonder long-lived. Also
that kind of obedience, which Tacitus speaketh
of, is to be held suspected : " Erant in officio,
sed tamen qui mallent mandata imperantium
interpretari, quam exequi ; " disputing, ex-
cusing, cavilling upon mandates and directions, is a kind of shaking off the yoke, and
assay of disobedience : especially if in those
disputings they which are for the direction
speak fearfully and tenderly, and those that are
against it, audaciously.

Also, as Machiavel noteth well, when princes,
that ought to be common parents, make them-

selves as a party, and lean to a side, that is, as
a boat that is overthrown by uneven weight on
the one side—as was well seen in the time of
Henry III. of France ; for, first himself entered
league for the extirpation of the Protestants,
and presently after the same league was turned
upon himself ; for when the authority of
princes is made but an accessory to a cause,
and that there be other bands that tie faster
than the band of sovereignty, kings begin to
be put almost out of possession.

Also, when discords, and quarrels, and factions are carried openly and audaciously ; it is
a sign the reverence of government is lost ; for
the motions of the greatest persons in a government ought to be as the motions of the planets
under *primum mobile* (according to the old
opinion), which is, that every of them is carried
swiftly by the highest motion, and softly in
their own motion ; and, therefore, when great
ones in their own particular motion move
violently, and, as Tacitus expresseth it well,
" Liberius quam ut imperantium meminissent "
—it is a sign the orbs are out of frame ; for reverence is that wherewith princes are girt from
God, who threateneth the dissolving thereof ;
" Solvam cingula regum."

So when any of the four pillars of government are mainly shaken, or weakened (which
are religion, justice, counsel, and treasure),

men had need to pray for fair weather. But let us pass from this part of predictions (concerning which, nevertheless, more light may be taken from that which followeth), and let us speak first of the materials of seditions, then of the motives of them, and thirdly of the remedies.

Concerning the materials of seditions, it is a thing well to be considered—for the surest way to prevent seditions (if the times do bear it) is to take away the matter of them ; for if there be fuel prepared, it is hard to tell whence the spark shall come that shall set it on fire. The matter of seditions is of two kinds, much poverty, and much discontentment. It is certain, so many overthrown estates, so many votes for troubles. Lucan noteth well the state of Rome before the civil war :—

" Hinc usura vorax, rapidumque in tempore fœnus,
    Hinc concussa fides, et multis utile bellum."

This same " multis utile bellum " is an assured and infallible sign of a State disposed to seditions and troubles ; and if this poverty and broken estate in the better sort be joined with a want and necessity in the mean people, the danger is imminent and great—for the rebellions of the belly are the worst. As for discontentments, they are in the politic body like to humours in the natural, which are apt to gather a preternatural heat, and to inflame ; and let no prince measure the danger of them by this, whether they be just or unjust—for that were to imagine people to be too reasonable, who do often spurn at their own good,—nor yet by this, whether the griefs whereupon they rise be in fact great or small ; for they are the most dangerous discontentments, where the fear is greater than the feeling : " Dolendi modus, timendi non item "—besides, in great oppressions, the same things that provoke the patience do withal mate the courage ; but in fears it is not so—neither let any prince, or State, be secure concerning discontentments, because they have been often, or have been long, and yet no peril hath ensued—for as it is true that every vapour or fume doth not turn into a storm, so it is nevertheless true that storms, though they blow over divers times, yet may fall at last ; and, as the Spanish proverb noteth well, " The cord breaketh at the last by the weakest pull."

The causes and motives of seditions are innovations in religion, taxes, alteration of laws and customs, breaking of privileges, general oppression, advancement of unworthy persons, strangers, deaths, disbanded soldiers, factions grown desperate ; and whatsoever in offending people joineth and knitteth them in a common cause.

For the remedies, there may be some general preservatives, whereof we will speak : as for the just cure, it must answer to the particular disease, and so be left to counsel rather than rule.

The first remedy or prevention is to remove, by all means possible, that material cause of sedition whereof we speak, which is, want and poverty in the estate : to which purpose serveth the opening and well-balancing of trade ; the cherishing of manufactures ; the banishing of idleness ; the repressing of waste and excess by sumptuary laws ; the improvement and husbanding of the soil ; the regulating of prices of things vendible ; the moderating of taxes and tributes ; and the like. Generally, it is to be foreseen that the population of a kingdom (especially if it be not mown down by wars) do not exceed the stock of the kingdom which should maintain them : neither is the population to be reckoned only by number, for a smaller number, that spend more and earn less, do wear out an estate sooner than a greater number that live low and gather more : therefore the multiplying of nobility, and other degrees of quality, in an over-proportion to the common people, doth speedily bring a State to necessity ; and so doth likewise an overgrown clergy, for they bring nothing to the stock ; and in like manner, when more are bred scholars than preferments can take off.

It is likewise to be remembered, that, forasmuch as the increase of any estate must be upon the foreigner (for whatsoever is somewhere gotten is somewhere lost), there be but three things which one nation selleth unto another—the commodity as nature yieldeth it, the manufacture, and the vecture, or carriage : so that, if these three wheels go, wealth will flow as in a spring tide. And it cometh many times to pass, that " materiam superabit opus "—that " the work and carriage is worth more than the material," and enricheth a State more ; as is notably seen in the Low Countrymen, who have the best mines above ground in the world.

Above all things, good policy is to be used, that the treasures and monies in a State be not gathered into few hands, for otherwise a State may have a great stock, and yet starve ; and money is like muck, not good except it be spread. This is done chiefly by suppressing, or, at the least, keeping a strait hand upon the devouring trades of usury, engrossing great pasturages and the like.

For removing discontentments, or, at least, the danger of them, there is in every State (as we know) two portions of subjects, the nobles and the commonalty. When one of these is discontent, the danger is not great; for common people are of slow motion, if they be not excited by the greater sort; and the greater sort are of small strength, except the multitude be apt and ready to move of themselves: then is the danger, when the greater sort do but wait for the troubling of the waters amongst the meaner, that then they may declare themselves. The poets feign that the rest of the gods would have bound Jupiter, which he hearing of, by the counsel of Pallas, sent for Briareus, with his hundred hands, to come in to his aid—an emblem, no doubt, to show how safe it is for monarchs to make sure of the good-will of common people.

To give moderate liberty for griefs and discontentments to evaporate (so it be without too great insolency or bravery) is a safe way; for he that turneth the humours back, and maketh the wound bleed inwards, endangereth malign ulcers and pernicious imposthumations.

The part of Epimetheus might well become Prometheus, in the case of discontentments; for there is not a better provision against them. Epimetheus, when griefs and evils flew abroad, at last shut the lid, and kept hope in the bottom of the vessel. Certainly, the politic and artificial nourishing and entertaining of hopes, and carrying men from hopes to hopes, is one of the best antidotes against the poison

of discontentments : and it is a certain sign of
a wise government and proceeding, when it
can hold men's hearts by hopes, when it cannot
by satisfaction ; and when it can handle things
in such manner as no evil shall appear so
peremptory but that it hath some outlet of
hope : which is the less hard to do, because
both particular persons and factions are apt
enough to flatter themselves, or, at least, to
brave that which they believe not.

Also the foresight and prevention, that there
be no likely or fit head whereupon discontented
persons may resort, and under whom they may
join, is a known, but an excellent point of
caution. I understand a fit head to be one
that hath greatness and reputation, that hath
confidence with the discontented party, and
upon whom they turn their eyes, and that is
thought discontented in his own particular ;
which kind of persons are either to be won
and reconciled to the State, and that in a fast
and true manner, or to be fronted with some
other of the same party that may oppose them,
and so divide the reputation. Generally, the
dividing and breaking of all factions and com-
binations that are adverse to the State, and
setting them at distance, or, at least, distrust
among themselves, is not one of the worst
remedies ; for it is a desperate case, if those
that hold with the proceeding of the State be

full of discord and faction, and those that are against it be entire and united.

I have noted that some witty and sharp speeches, which have fallen from princes, have given fire to seditions. Cæsar did himself infinite hurt in that speech, " Sylla nescivit literas, non potuit dictare ; " for it did utterly cut off that hope which men had entertained, that he would at one time or other give over his dictatorship. Galba undid himself by that speech, " Legi a se militem, non emi ; " for it put the soldiers out of hope of the donative. Probus, likewise, by that speech, " Si vixero, non opus erit amplius Romano imperio militibus ; " a speech of great despair for the soldiers ; and many the like. Surely princes had need, in tender matter and ticklish times, to beware what they say, especially in these short speeches, which fly abroad like darts, and are thought to be shot out of their secret intentions ; for, as for large discourses, they are flat things, and not so much noted.

Lastly, let princes, against all events, not be without some great person, one or rather more, of military valour, near unto them, for the repressing of seditions in their·beginnings ; for, without that, there useth to be more trepidation in court upon the first breaking out of trouble than were fit ; and the State runneth the danger of that which Tacitus saith—" Atque is habitus animorum fuit, ut pessimum facinus auderent pauci, plures vellent, omnes paterentur;" but let such military persons be assured and well reputed of, rather than factious and popular—holding also good correspondence with the other great men in the State, or else the remedy is worse than the disease.

XVI

OF ATHEISM

I HAD rather believe all the fables in the
Legend, and the Talmud, and the Alcoran,
than that this universal frame is without a
mind ; and, therefore, God never wrought
miracles to convince atheism, because his ordinary works convince it. It is true that a little
philosophy inclineth Man's mind to atheism,
but depth in philosophy bringeth men's minds
about to religion ; for while the mind of Man
looketh upon second causes scattered, it may
sometimes rest in them, and go no farther ; but
when it beholdeth the chain of them confederate, and linked together, it must needs fly
to Providence and Deity : nay, even that school
which is most accused of atheism doth most
demonstrate religion ; that is, the school of
Leucippus, and Democritus, and Epicurus—
for it is a thousand times more credible that
four mutable elements and one immutable fifth
essence, duly and eternally placed, need no

God, than that an army of infinite small portions, or seeds unplaced, should have produced this order and beauty without a divine marshal. The Scripture saith, " The fool hath said in his heart, there is no God ; " it is not said, " The fool hath thought in his heart ; " so as he rather saith it by rote to himself, as that he would have, than that he can thoroughly believe it, or be persuaded of it ; for none deny there is a God, but those for whom it maketh that there were no God. It appeareth in nothing more that atheism is rather in the lip than in the heart of Man, than by this, that atheists will ever be talking of that their opinion, as if they fainted in it themselves, and would be glad to be strengthened by the consent of others ; nay, more, you shall have atheists strive to get disciples, as it fareth with other sects ; and, which is most of all, you shall have them that will suffer for atheism, and not recant : whereas, if they did truly think that there were no such thing as God, why should they trouble themselves ? Epicurus is charged that he did but dissemble for his credit's sake when he affirmed there were blest natures, but such as enjoy themselves without having respect to the government of the world, wherein they say he did temporize, though in secret he thought there was no God ; but certainly he is traduced, for his words are noble and divine ;

" Non deos vulgi negare profanum : sed vulgi opiniones diis applicare profanum." Plato could have said no more ; and although he had the confidence to deny the administration, he had not the power to deny the nature. The Indians of the West have names for their particular gods, though they have no name for God ; as if the heathens should have had the names Jupiter, Apollo, Mars, &c., but not the word Deus ; which shows, that even those barbarous people have the notion, though they have not the latitude and extent of it ; so that against atheists the very savages take part with the very subtilest philosophers. The contemplative atheist is rare—a Diagoras, a Bion, a Lucian, perhaps, and some others : and yet they seem to be more than they are, for that all that impugn a received religion, or superstition, are, by the adverse part, branded with the name of atheists ; but the great atheists indeed are hypocrites, which are ever handling holy things, but without feeling, so as they must needs be cauterized in the end.

The causes of atheism are, divisions in religion, if there be many ; for any one main division addeth zeal to both sides, but many divisions introduce atheism : another is, scandal of priests, when it is come to that which St. Bernard saith, " Non est jam dicere, ut populus, sic sacerdos ; quia nec sic populus,

ut sacerdos." A third is, a custom of profane
scoffing in holy matters, which doth by little
and little deface the reverence of religion :
and lastly, learned times, especially with peace
and prosperity ; for troubles and adversities
do more bow men's minds to religion. They
that deny a God destroy a man's nobility, for
certainly Man is of kin to the beasts by his
body ; and if he be not of kin to God by his
spirit, he is a base and ignoble creature. It
destroys likewise magnanimity, and the raising
human nature ; for, take an example of a dog,
and mark what a generosity and courage he
will put on when he finds himself maintained
by a man, who to him is instead of a God,
or *melior natura*—which courage is manifestly
such as that creature, without that confidence
of a better nature than his own, could never
attain. So man, when he resteth and assureth
himself upon divine protection and favour,
gathereth a force and faith which human
nature in itself could not obtain ; therefore, as
atheism is in all respects hateful, so in this,
that it depriveth human nature of the means to
exalt itself above human frailty. As it is in
particular persons, so it is in nations :—never
was there such a state for magnanimity as
Rome. Of this state hear what Cicero saith :
" Quam volumus, licet, patres conscripti, nos
amemus, tamen nec numero Hispanos, nec

robore Gallos, nec calliditate Pœnos, nec artibus Græcos, nec denique hoc ipso hujus gentis et terræ domestico nativoque sensu Italos ipsos et Latinos ; sed pietate, ac religione, atque hac una sapientia, quod deorum immortalium numine omnia regi, gubernarique perspeximus, omnes gentes nationesque superavimus."

XVII

OF SUPERSTITION

IT were better to have no opinion of God at all, than such an opinion as is unworthy of Him ; for the one is unbelief, the other is contumely : and certainly superstition is the reproach of the Deity. Plutarch saith well to that purpose : " Surely," saith he, " I had rather a great deal men should say there was no such a man at all as Plutarch, than that they should say there was one Plutarch, that would eat his children as soon as they were born " ; as the poets speak of Saturn : and as the contumely is greater towards God, so the danger is greater towards men. Atheism leaves a man to sense, to philosophy, to natural piety, to laws, to reputation—all which may be guides to an outward moral virtue, though religion were not,—but superstition dismounts all these, and erecteth an absolute monarchy in the minds of men ; therefore atheism did never perturb States ; for it makes men wary of themselves, as looking no further; and we see the times inclined to atheism, as the time of Augustus Cæsar, were civil times; but superstition hath been the confusion of many States, and bringeth in a new *primum mobile*, that ravisheth all the spheres of government. The master of superstition is the people, and in all superstition wise men follow fools; and arguments are fitted to practice in a reversed order. It was gravely said, by some of the prelates in the Council of Trent, where the doctrine of the schoolmen bare great sway, that the schoolmen were like astronomers, which did feign eccentrics and epicycles, and such engines of orbs, to save the phenomena, though they knew there were no such things; and, in like manner, that the schoolmen had framed a number of subtile and intricate axioms and theorems, to save the practice of the Church.

The causes of superstition are pleasing and sensual rites and ceremonies; excess of outward and pharisaical holiness; over-great reverence of traditions, which cannot but load the Church; the stratagems of prelates for their own ambition and lucre; the favouring too much of good intentions, which openeth the gate to conceits and novelties; the taking an aim at divine matters by human, which cannot but breed mixture of imaginations; and, lastly, barbarous times, especially joined with calamities and disasters. Superstition, without a veil, is a deformed thing; for as it addeth deformity to an ape to be so like a man, so the similitude of superstition to religion makes it the more deformed; and as wholesome meat corrupteth to little worms, so good forms and orders corrupt into a number of petty observances. There is a superstition in avoiding superstition, when men think to do best if they go farthest from the superstition formerly received; therefore care would be had that (as it fareth in ill purgings) the good be not taken away with the bad, which commonly is done when the people is the reformer.

XVIII

OF TRAVEL

TRAVEL, in the younger sort, is a part of education; in the elder, a part of experience. He that travelleth into a country, before he hath some entrance into the language, goeth to school, and not to travel. That young men travel under some tutor, or grave servant, I allow well; so that he be such a one that hath the language, and hath been in the country before; whereby he may be able to tell them what things are worthy to be seen in the country where they go, what acquaintances they are to seek, what exercises or discipline the place yieldeth; for else young men shall go hooded, and look abroad little. It is a strange thing that, in sea voyages, where there is nothing to be seen but sky and sea, men should make diaries; but in land-travel, wherein so much is to be observed, for the most part they omit it—as if chance were fitter to be registered than observation: let diaries, therefore, be brought in use. The things to be seen and observed are the courts of princes, especially when they give audience to ambassadors ; the courts of justice, while they sit and hear causes ; and so of consistories ecclesiastic ; the churches and monasteries, with the monuments which are therein extant ; the walls and fortifications of cities and towns ; and so the havens and harbours, antiquities and ruins, libraries, colleges, disputations and lectures, where any are ; shipping and navies ; houses and gardens of state and pleasure near great cities ; armories, arsenals, magazines, exchanges, burses, warehouses, exercises of horsemanship, fencing, training of soldiers, and the like ; comedies, such whereunto the better sort of persons do resort ; treasuries of jewels and robes ; cabinets and rarities ; and, to conclude, whatsoever is memorable in the places where they go—after all which, the tutors or servants ought to make diligent inquiry. As for triumphs, masks, feasts, weddings, funerals, capital executions, and such shows, men need not be put in mind of them ; yet they are not to be neglected. If you will have a young man to put his travel into a little room, and in short time to gather much, this you must do : first, as was said, he must have some entrance into the language before he goeth ; then he must have such a servant, or tutor, as knoweth the country, as was likewise said ; let him carry with him also some card, or book describing the country where he travelleth, which will be a good key to his inquiry ; let him keep also a diary ; let him not stay long in one city or town, more or less as the place deserveth, but not long; nay, when he stayeth in one city or town, let him change his lodging from one end and part of the town to another, which is a great adamant of acquaintance ; let him sequester himself from the company of his countrymen, and diet in such places where there is good company of the nation where he travelleth ; let him, upon his removes from one place to another, procure recommendation to some person of quality residing in the place whither he removeth, that he may use his favour in those things he desireth to see or know ; thus he may abridge his travel with much profit.

As for the acquaintance which is to be sought in travel, that which is most of all profitable is acquaintance with the secretaries and employed men of ambassadors ; for so in travelling in one country he shall suck the experience of many. Let him also see and visit eminent persons in all kinds, which are of great name abroad, that he may be able to tell how the life agreeth with the fame ; for quarrels, they are with care and discretion to be avoided—

they are commonly for mistresses, healths, place, and words : and let a man beware how he keepeth company with choleric and quarrelsome persons, for they will engage him into their own quarrels. When a traveller returneth home, let him not leave the countries where he hath travelled altogether behind him, but maintain a correspondence by letters with those of his acquaintance which are of most worth ; and let his travel appear rather in his discourse than in his apparel or gesture ; and in his discourse let him be rather advised in his answers than forward to tell stories : and let it appear that he doth not change his country manners for those of foreign parts, but only prick in some flowers of that he hath learned abroad into the customs of his own country.

XIX

OF EMPIRE

IT is a miserable state of mind to have few things to desire, and many things to fear; and yet that commonly is the case with kings, who being at the highest, want matter of desire, which makes their minds more languishing, and have many representations of perils and shadows, which make their minds the less clear: and this is one reason also of that effect which the Scripture speaketh of, "That the king's heart is inscrutable;" for multitude of jealousies, and lack of some predominant desire, that should marshal and put in order all the rest, maketh any man's heart hard to find or sound. Hence it comes likewise, that princes many times make themselves desires, and set their hearts upon toys; sometimes upon a building; sometimes upon erecting of an Order; sometimes upon the advancing of a person; sometimes upon obtaining excellency in some art, or feat of the hand—as Nero for

4

playing on the harp ; Domitian for certainty of the hand with the arrow ; Commodus for playing at fence ; Caracalla for driving chariots ; and the like. This seemeth incredible unto those that know not the principle, that the mind of Man is more cheered and refreshed by profiting in small things, than by standing at a stay in great. We see also that kings that have been fortunate conquerors in their first years, it being not possible for them to go forward infinitely, but that they must have some check or arrest in their fortunes, turn in their latter years to be superstitious and melancholy ; as did Alexander the Great, Diocletian, and in our memory Charles V., and others ; for he that is used to go forward, and findeth a stop, falleth out of his own favour, and is not the thing he was.

To speak now of the true temper of empire, it is a thing rare and hard to keep, for both temper and distemper consist of contraries ; but it is one thing to mingle contraries, another to interchange them. The answer of Apollonius to Vespasian is full of excellent instruction. Vespasian asked him, " What was Nero's overthrow ? " He answered, " Nero could touch and tune the harp well, but in government sometimes he used to wind the pins too high, sometimes to let them down too low ; " and certain it is, that nothing destroyeth authority so much as the unequal and untimely interchange, of power pressed too far, and relaxed too much.

This is true, that the wisdom of all these latter times in princes' affairs is rather fine deliveries, and shiftings of dangers and mischiefs, when they are near, than solid and grounded courses to keep them aloof; but this is but to try masteries with fortune; and let men beware how they neglect and suffer matter of trouble to be prepared; for no man can forbid the spark, nor tell whence it may come. The difficulties in princes' business are many and great, but the greatest difficulty is often in their own mind; for it is common with princes (saith Tacitus) to will contradictories: " Sunt plerumque regum voluntates vehementes, et inter se contrariæ." For it is the solecism of power to think to command the end, and yet not to endure the mean.

Kings have to deal with their neighbours, their wives, their children, their prelates or clergy, their nobles, their second nobles or gentlemen, their merchants, their commons, and their men of war; and from all these arise dangers, if care and circumspection be not used.

First, for their neighbours, there can no general rule be given (the occasions are so variable), save one which ever holdeth—which is, that princes do keep due sentinel, that none of their neighbours do overgrow so (by increase of territory, by embracing of trade, by approaches, or the like), as they become more able to annoy them than they were ; and this is generally the work of standing councils to foresee and to hinder it. During that triumvirate of kings, King Henry VIII. of England, Francis I., king of France, and Charles V., emperor, there was such a watch kept that none of the three could win a palm of ground, but the other two would straightways balance it, either by confederation, or, if need were, by a war, and would not in any wise take up peace at interest ; and the like was done by that league (which Guicciardini saith was the security of Italy), made between Ferdinando, king of Naples, Lorenzius Medices, and Ludovicus Sforsa, potentates, the one of Florence, the other of Milan. Neither is the opinion of some of the schoolmen to be received, that a war cannot justly be made, but upon a precedent injury or provocation ; for there is no question but a just fear of an imminent danger, though there be no blow given, is a lawful cause of war.

For their wives, there are cruel examples of them. Livia is infamed for the poisoning of her husband ; Roxolana, Solyman's wife, was the destruction of that renowned prince, Sultan

Mustapha, and otherwise troubled his house and succession; Edward II. of England's queen had the principal hand in the deposing and murder of her husband. This kind of danger is then to be feared chiefly when the wives have plots for the raising of their own children or else that they be advoutresses.

For their children, the tragedies likewise of dangers from them have been many; and generally the entering of the fathers into suspicion of their children hath been ever unfortunate. The destruction of Mustapha (that we named before) was so fatal to Solyman's line, as the succession of the Turks from Solyman until this day is suspected to be untrue, and of strange blood, for that Selymus II. was thought to be suppositious. The destruction of Crispus, a young prince of rare towardness, by Constantinus the Great, his father, was in like manner fatal to his house, for both Constantinus and Constance, his sons, died violent deaths; and Constantius, his other son, did little better, who died indeed of sickness, but after that Julianus had taken arms against him. The destruction of Demetrius, son to Philip II. of Macedon, turned upon the father, who died of repentance: and many like examples there are, but few or none where the fathers had good by such distrust, except it were where the sons were in open arms against them, as

was Selymus I. against Bajazet, and the three
sons of Henry II., king of England.

For their prelates, when they are proud and
great, there is also danger from them; as it
was in the times of Anselmus and Thomas
Beckett, archbishops of Canterbury, who, with
their crosiers, did almost try it with the king's
sword; and yet they had to deal with stout
and haughty kings—William Rufus, Henry I.,
and Henry II. The danger is not from that
estate, but where it hath a dependence of
foreign authority, or where the churchmen
come in and are elected, not by the collation
of the king, or particular patrons, but by the
people.

For their nobles, to keep them at a distance,
it is not amiss; but to depress them may make
a king more absolute, but less safe, and less
able to perform anything that he desires. I
have noted it in my history of King Henry VII.
of England, who depressed his nobility, whereupon it came to pass that his times were full
of difficulties and troubles; for the nobility,
though they continued loyal unto him, yet did
they not co-operate with him in his business—
so that in effect he was fain to do all things
himself.

For their second nobles, there is not much
danger from them, being a body dispersed:
they may sometimes discourse high, but that

doth little hurt ; besides, they are a counterpoise to the higher nobility, that they grow not too potent ; and, lastly, being the most immediate in authority with the common people, they do best temper popular commotions.

For their merchants, they are *vena porta*, and if they flourish not, a kingdom may have good limbs, but will have empty veins, and nourish little. Taxes and imposts upon them do seldom good to the king's revenue, for that which he wins in the hundred he loseth in the shire : the particular rates being increased, but the total bulk of trading rather decreased.

For their commons, there is little danger from them, except it be where they have great and potent heads, or where you meddle with the point of religion, or their customs, or means of life.

For their men of war, it is a dangerous state where they live and remain in a Body, and are used to donatives, whereof we see examples in the Janizaries and pretorian bands of Rome ; but trainings of men, and arming them in several places, and under several commanders, and without donatives, are things of defence, and no danger.

Princes are like to heavenly bodies, which cause good or evil times ; and which have much veneration, but no rest. All precepts concerning kings are in effect comprehended in those two remembrances: "Memento quod es homo," and "Memento quod es Deus," or "vice Dei"—the one bridleth their power, and the other their will.

XX

OF COUNSEL

THE greatest trust between man and man is the trust of giving counsel; for in other confidences men commit the parts of life, their lands, their goods, their children, their credit, some particular affair; but to such as they make their counsellors they commit the whole —by how much the more they are obliged to all faith and integrity. The wisest princes need not think it any diminution to their greatness, or derogation to their sufficiency, to rely upon counsel. God himself is not without, but hath made it one of the great names of the blessed Son, the " Counsellor." Solomon hath pronounced that " in counsel is stability." Things will have their first or second agitation; if they be not tossed upon the arguments of counsel, they will be tossed upon the waves of fortune, and be full of inconstancy, doing and undoing, like the reeling of a drunken man. Solomon's son found the force of counsel, as his father saw the necessity of it: for the beloved kingdom of God was first rent and broken by ill counsel—upon which counsel there are set for our instruction the two marks whereby bad counsel is for ever best discerned, that it was young counsel for the persons, and violent counsel for the matter.

The ancient times do set forth in figure both the incorporation and inseparable conjunction of counsel with Kings, and the wise and politic use of counsel by Kings; the one, in that they say Jupiter did marry Metis, which signifieth counsel, whereby they intend that sovereignty is married to counsel; the other in that which followeth, which was thus:—they say, after Jupiter was married to Metis, she conceived by him and was with child, but Jupiter suffered her not to stay till she brought forth, but ate her up, whereby he became himself with child, and was delivered of Pallas armed out of his head. Which monstrous fable containeth a secret of empire how kings are to make use of their counsel of state—that first, they ought to refer matters unto them, which is the first begetting or impregnation; but when they are elaborate, moulded, and shaped in the womb of their council, and grow ripe and ready to be brought forth, that then they suffer not their council to go through with the resolution and direction, as if it depended on them, but take the matter back into their own hands, and make it appear to the world, that the decrees and final directions (which, because they come forth with prudence and power, are resembled to Pallas armed) proceeded from themselves, and not only from their authority, but (the more to add reputation to themselves) from their head and device.

Let us now speak of the inconveniences of counsel, and of the remedies. The inconveniences that have been noted in calling and using counsel are three :—first, the revealing of affairs, whereby they become less secret ; secondly, the weakening of the authority of princes, as if they were less of themselves ; thirdly, the danger of being unfaithfully counselled, and more for the good of them that counsel than of him that is counselled—for which inconveniences, the doctrine of Italy, and practice of France, in some kings' times, hath introduced cabinet councils—a remedy worse than the disease.

As to secrecy, princes are not bound to communicate all matters with all counsellors, but may extract and select—neither is it necessary that he that consulteth what he should do should declare what he will do ; but let princes beware that the unsecreting of their affairs comes not from themselves : and as for cabinet councils, it may be their motto, " Plenus rimarum sum." One futile person, that maketh it his glory to tell, will do more hurt than many that know it their duty to conceal. It is true there be some affairs which require extreme secrecy, which will hardly go beyond one or two persons besides the king—neither are those counsels unprosperous,—for, besides the secrecy, they commonly go on constantly in one spirit of direction without distraction ; but then it must be a prudent king, such as is able to grind with a hand-mill—and those inward counsellors had need also be wise men, and especially true and trusty to the king's ends, as it was with King Henry VII. of England, who in his greatest business imparted himself to none, except it were to Morton and Fox.

For weakness of authority the fable showeth the remedy—nay, the majesty of kings is rather exalted than diminished when they are in the chair of council,—neither was there ever prince bereaved of his dependencies by his council, except where there hath been either an over-greatness in one counsellor, or an over-strict combination in divers, which are things soon found and holpen.

For the last inconvenience, that men will counsel with an eye to themselves ; certainly, " Non inveniet fidem super terram," is meant of the nature of times, and not of all particular persons. There be that are in nature faithful and sincere, and plain and direct, not crafty and involved—let princes, above all, draw to themselves such natures. Besides, counsellors are not commonly so united but that one counsellor keepeth sentinel over another : so that if any counsel out of faction or private ends, it commonly comes to the king's ear : but the best remedy is, if princes know their counsellors, as well as their counsellors know them :—

" Principis est virtus maxima nosse suos."

And on the other side, counsellors should not be too speculative into their sovereign's person. The true composition of a counsellor is rather to be skilful in their master's business than in his nature : for then he is like to advise him, and not to feed his humour. It is of singular use to princes if they take the opinions of their council both separately and together ; for private opinion is more free, but opinion before others is more reverend. In private, men are more bold in their own humours, and, in consort, men are more obnoxious to others' humours, therefore it is good to take both— and of the inferior sort, rather in private to preserve freedom,—of the greater, rather in consort to preserve respect. It is in vain for princes to take counsel concerning matters if they take no counsel likewise concerning persons—for all matters are as dead images, and the life of the execution of affairs resteth in the good choice of persons; neither is it enough to consult concerning persons, " secundum genera " as in an idea of mathematical description, what the kind and character of the person should be ; for the greatest errors are committed, and the most judgment is shown, in the choice of individuals. It was truly said, " Optimi consiliarii mortui "—" Books will speak plain when counsellors blanch," therefore it is good to be conversant in them, specially the books of such as themselves have been the actors upon the stage.

The councils at this day in most places are but familiar meetings, where matters are rather talked on than debated ; and they run too swift to the order or act of counsel. It were better that, in causes of weight, the matter were propounded one day, and not spoken to till next day, " in nocte consilium " ; so was it done in the commission of union between England and Scotland, which was a grave and orderly assembly. I commend set days for petitions ; for both it gives the suitors more certainty for their attendance, and it frees the meetings for matters of estate, that they may " hoc agere." In choice of committees for ripening business for the council, it is better to chuse indifferent persons, than to make an indifferency by putting in those that are strong on both sides. I commend also standing commissions ; as for trade, for treasure, for war, for suits, for some provinces ; for where there be divers particular councils, and but one council of estate (as it is in Spain), they are, in effect, no more than standing commissions, save that they have greater authority. Let such as are to inform councils out of their particular professions (as lawyers, seamen, mintmen, and the like) be first heard before committees, and then, as occasion serves, before the council ; and let them not come in multitudes, or in a tribunitious manner, for that is to clamour councils, not to inform them. A long table and a square table, or seats about the walls, seem things of form, but are things of substance ; for at a long table, a few at the upper end, in effect, sway all the business ; but in the other form there is more use of the counsellors' opinions that sit lower. A king, when he presides in council, let him beware how he opens his own inclination too much in that which he propoundeth ; for else counsellors will but take the wind of him, and instead of giving free counsel, will sing him a song of " placebo."

XXI

OF DELAYS

FORTUNE is like the market, where, many times, if you can stay a little, the price will fall; and again, it is sometimes like Sibylla's offer, which at first offereth the commodity at full, then consumeth part and part, and still holdeth up the price; for occasion (as it is in the common verse) turneth a bald noddle after she hath presented her locks in front, and no hold taken; or, at least, turneth the handle of the bottle first to be received, and after the belly, which is hard to clasp. There is surely no greater wisdom than well to time the beginnings and onsets of things. Dangers are no more light, if they once seem light; and more dangers have deceived men than forced them: nay, it were better to meet some dangers halfway, though they come nothing near, than to keep too long a watch upon their approaches; for if a man watch too long, it is odds he will fall asleep. On the other side, to be deceived with too long shadows (as some have been when the moon was low, and shone on their enemies' backs), and so to shoot off before the time, or to teach dangers to come on, by over-early buckling towards them, is another extreme. The ripeness or unripeness of the occasion (as we said) must ever be well weighed; and generally it is good to commit the beginnings of all great actions to Argus with his hundred eyes, and the ends to Briareus with his hundred hands—first to watch, and then to speed; for the helmet of Pluto, which maketh the politic man go invisible, is secrecy in the counsel, and celerity in the execution; for when things are once come to the execution, there is no secrecy comparable to celerity—like the motion of a bullet in the air, which flieth so swift as it outruns the eye.

XXII

OF CUNNING

WE take cunning for a sinister, or crooked wisdom; and certainly there is a great difference between a cunning man and a wise man, not only in point of honesty, but in point of ability. There be that can pack the cards, and yet cannot play well; so there are some that are good in canvasses and factions, that are otherwise weak men. Again, it is one thing to understand persons and another thing to understand matters; for many are perfect in men's humours that are not greatly capable of the real part of business, which is the constitution of one that hath studied men more than books. Such men are fitter for practice than for counsel, and they are good but in their own alley: turn them to new men, and they have lost their aim; so as the old rule, to know a fool from a wise man, " Mitte ambos nudos ad ignotos, et videbis," doth scarce hold for them. And because these cunning men are like haberdashers of small wares, it is not amiss to set forth their shop.

It is a point of cunning to wait upon him with whom you speak, with your eye, as the Jesuits give it in precept—for there be many wise men that have secret hearts and transparent countenances ; yet this would be done with a demure abasing of your eye sometimes, as the Jesuits also do use.

Another is, that when you have any thing to obtain of present dispatch, you entertain and amuse the party with whom you deal with some other discourse, that he be not too much awake to make objections. I knew a counsellor and secretary that never came to Queen Elizabeth of England with bills to sign but he would always first put her into some discourse of state, that she might the less mind the bills.

The like surprise may be made by moving things when the party is in haste, and cannot stay to consider advisedly of that is moved.

If a man would cross a business that he doubts some other would handsomely and effectually move, let him pretend to wish it well, and move it himself, in such sort as may foil it.

The breaking off in the midst of that one was about to say, as if he took himself up, breeds a greater appetite in him with whom you confer to know more.

And because it works better when anything seemeth to be gotten from you by question, than if you offer it of yourself, you may lay a bait for a question by showing another visage and countenance than you are wont; to the end, to give occasion for the party to ask what the matter is of the change, as Nehemiah did, —" And I had not before that time been sad before the king."

In things that are tender and unpleasing, it is good to break the ice by some whose words are of less weight, and to reserve the more weighty voice to come in as by chance, so that he may be asked the question upon the other's speech; as Narcissus did, in relating to Claudius the marriage of Messalina and Silius.

In things that a man would not be seen in himself, it is a point of cunning to borrow the name of the world; as to say, " The world says," or, " There is a speech abroad."

I knew one that, when he wrote a letter, he would put that which was most material in the postcript, as if it had been a bye matter.

I knew another that, when he came to have speech, he would pass over that he intended most, and go forth, and come back again, and speak of it as a thing he had almost forgot.

Some procure themselves to be surprised at such times as it is like the party, that they work upon, will suddenly come upon them,

and be found with a letter in their hand, or
doing somewhat which they are not accustomed, to the end they may be apposed of
those things which of themselves they are
desirous to utter.

It is a point of cunning to let fall those
words in a man's own name which he would
have another man learn and use, and thereupon
take advantage. I knew two that were competitors for the secretary's place in Queen
Elizabeth's time, and yet kept good quarter
between themselves, and would confer one
with another upon the business ; and the one
of them said that to be a secretary in the
declination of a monarchy was a ticklish thing,
and that he did not affect it ; the other straight
caught up those words, and discoursed with
divers of his friends, that he had no reason
to desire to be secretary in the declining of
a monarchy. The first man took hold of it,
and found means it was told the queen ; who,
hearing of a declination of monarchy, took it
so ill, as she would never after hear of the
other's suit.

There is a cunning, which we in England
call " the turning of the cat in the pan " ;
which is, when that which a man says to
another, he lays it as if another had said it to
him ; and, to say truth, it is not easy, when
such a matter passed between two, to make it

appear from which of them it first moved and began.

It is a way that some men have, to glance and dart at others by justifying themselves by negatives; as to say, "This I do not"; as Tigellinus did towards Burrhus, saying, "Se non diversas spes, sed incolumitatem imperatoris simpliciter spectare."

Some have in readiness so many tales and stories, as there is nothing they would insinuate but they can wrap it into a tale; which serveth both to keep themselves more in guard, and to make others carry it with more pleasure.

It is a good point of cunning for a man to shape the answer he would have in his own words and propositions, for it makes the other party stick the less.

It is strange how long some men will lie in wait to speak somewhat they desire to say, and how far about they will fetch, and how many other matters they will beat over to come near it; it is a thing of great patience, but yet of much use.

A sudden, bold, and unexpected question doth many times surprise a man, and lay him open. Like to him that, having changed his name, and walking in Paul's, another suddenly came behind him, and called him by his true name, whereat straightways he looked back.

But these small wares and petty points of

cunning are infinite, and it were a good deed to make a list of them ; for that nothing doth more hurt in a State than that cunning men pass for wise.

But certainly some there are that know the resorts and falls of business, that cannot sink into the main of it ; like a house that hath convenient stairs and entries, but never a fair room : therefore you shall see them find out pretty looses in the conclusion, but are no ways able to examine or debate matters ; and yet commonly they take advantage of their inability, and would be thought wits of direction. Some build rather upon the abusing of others, and (as we now say) putting tricks upon them, than upon the soundness of their own proceedings ; but Solomon saith, " Prudens advertit ad gressus suos ; stultus divertit ad dolos."

XXIII

OF WISDOM FOR A MAN'S SELF

AN ant is a wise creature for itself, but it is a shrewd thing in an orchard or garden; and certainly men that are great lovers of themselves waste the public. Divide with reason between self-love and society; and be so true to thyself as thou be not false to others, especially to thy king and country. It is a poor centre of a man's actions, himself. It is right earth; for that only stands fast upon his own centre; whereas all things that have affinity with the heavens move upon the centre of another, which they benefit. The referring of all to a man's self is more tolerable in a sovereign prince, because themselves are not only themselves, but their good and evil is at the peril of the public fortune: but it is a desperate evil in a servant to a prince, or a citizen in a republic; for whatsoever affairs pass such a man's hands, he crooketh them to his own ends, which must needs be often eccentric, to the ends of his master or State : therefore, let princes or States chuse such servants as have not this mark, except they mean their service should be made but the accessary. That which maketh the effect more pernicious is that all proportion is lost. It were disproportion enough for the servant's good to be preferred before the master's ; but yet it is a greater extreme when a little good of the servant shall carry things against the great good of the master's : and yet that is the case of bad officers, treasurers, ambassadors, generals, and other false and corrupt servants, which set a bias upon their bowl, of their own petty ends and envies, to the overthrow of their master's great and important affairs. And for the most part, the good such servants receive is after the model of their own fortune, but the hurt they sell for that good is after the model of their master's fortune. And certainly it is the nature of extreme self-lovers, as they will set a house on fire and it were but to roast their eggs ; and yet these men many times hold credit with their masters, because their study is but to please them, and profit themselves ; and for either respect they will abandon the good of their affairs.

Wisdom for a man's self is, in many branches thereof, a depraved thing : it is the wisdom of rats, that will be sure to leave a house some time before its fall : it is the wisdom of the fox, that thrusts out the badger, who digged and made room for him : it is the wisdom of crocodiles, that shed tears when they would devour. But that which is specially to be noted is that those which (as Cicero says of Pompey) are " sui amantes sine rivali " are many times unfortunate ; and whereas they have all their time sacrificed to themselves, they become in the end themselves sacrifices to the inconstancy of fortune, whose wings they thought by their self-wisdom to have pinioned.

XXIV

OF INNOVATIONS

As the births of living creatures at first are ill-shapen, so are all innovations, which are the births of time ; yet, notwithstanding, as those that first bring honour into their family are commonly more worthy than most that succeed, so the first precedent (if it be good) is seldom attained by imitation : for ill, to man's nature as it stands perverted, hath a natural motion, strongest in continuance ; but good, as a forced motion, strongest at first. Surely every medicine is an innovation, and he that will not apply new remedies must expect new evils : for time is the greatest innovator ; and if time of course alters things to the worse, and wisdom and counsel shall not alter them to the better, what shall be the end ? It is true that what is settled by custom, though it be not good, yet at least it is fit ; and those things which have long gone together, are, as it were, confederate with themselves ; whereas new

things piece not so well; but, though they
help by their utility, yet they trouble by their
inconformity; besides, they are like strangers,
more admired, and less favoured. All this is
true, if time stood still; which, contrariwise,
moveth so round, that a froward retention of
custom is as turbulent a thing as an innovation; and they that reverence too much old
times are but a scorn to the new. It were
good, therefore, that men in their innovations
would follow the example of time itself, which
indeed innovateth greatly, but quietly, and by
degrees scarce to be perceived; for otherwise,
whatsoever is new is unlooked for—and ever
it mends some, and pairs others; and he that
is holpen takes it for a fortune, and thanks the
time; and he that is hurt, for a wrong, and
imputeth it to the author. It is good also not
to try experiments in States, except the necessity be urgent, or the utility evident; and well
to beware that it be the reformation that
draweth on the change, and not the desire of
change that pretendeth the reformation: and
lastly, that the novelty, though it be not rejected, yet be held for a suspect; and, as the
Scripture saith, "That we make a stand upon
the ancient way, and then look about us, and
discover what is the straight and right way, and
so to walk in it."

XXV

OF DISPATCH

AFFECTED dispatch is one of the most dangerous
things to business that can be : it is like that
which the physicians call predigestion, or hasty
digestion, which is sure to fill the body full of
crudities, and secret seeds of diseases ; therefore, measure not dispatch by the time of sitting, but by the advancement of the business :
and as in races it is not the large stride, or high
lift, that makes the speed, so in business, the
keeping close to the matter, and not taking of
it too much at once, procureth dispatch. It is
the care of some, only to come off speedily for
the time, or to contrive some false periods of
business, because they may seem men of dispatch : but it is one thing to abbreviate by
contracting, another by cutting off ; and business so handled at several sittings or meetings
goeth commonly backward and forward in an
unsteady manner. I knew a wise man that
had it for a by-word, when he saw men hasten

to a conclusion, " Stay a little, that we may make an end the sooner."

On the other side, true dispatch is a rich thing ; for time is the measure of business, as money is of wares ; and business is bought at a dear hand where there is small dispatch. The Spartans and Spaniards have been noted to be of small dispatch : " Mi venga la muerte de Spagna," for then it will be sure to be long in coming.

Give good hearing to those that give the first information in business ; and rather direct them in the beginning than interrupt them in the continuance of their speeches ; for he that is put out of his own order will go forward and backward, and be more tedious while he waits upon his memory, than he could have been if he had gone on in his own course. But sometimes it is seen that the moderator is more troublesome than the actor.

Iterations are commonly loss of time : but there is no such gain of time as to iterate often the state of the question ; for it chaseth away many a frivolous speech as it is coming forth. Long and curious speeches are as fit for dispatch as a robe or mantle with a long train is for a race. Prefaces, and passages, and excusations, and other speeches of reference to the person, are great wastes of time ; and though they seem to proceed of modesty, they are bravery. Yet beware of being too material when there is any impediment or obstruction in men's wills ; for preoccupation of mind ever requireth preface of speech, like a fomentation to make the unguent enter.

Above all things, order and distribution, and singling out of parts, is the life of dispatch, so as the distribution be not too subtle ; for he that doth not divide will never enter well into business, and he that divideth too much will never come out of it clearly. To chuse time is to save time ; and an unseasonable motion is but beating the air. There be three parts of business—the preparation, the debate, or examination, and the perfection,—whereof, if you look for dispatch, let the middle only be the work of many, and the first and last the work of few. The proceeding upon somewhat conceived in writing doth for the most part facilitate dispatch ; for though it should be wholly rejected, yet that negative is more pregnant of direction than an indefinite, as ashes are more generative than dust.

XXVI

OF SEEMING WISE

IT hath been an opinion that the French are wiser than they seem, and the Spaniards seem wiser than they are ; but howsoever it be between nations, certainly it is so between man and man ; for, as the Apostle saith of godliness, " Having a show of godliness, but denying the power thereof,"—so certainly there are, in points of wisdom and sufficiency, that do nothing or little, very solemnly, *Magno conatu nugas*. It is a ridiculous thing, and fit for a satire to persons of judgment, to see what shifts these formalists have, and what prospectives to make superfices to seem body that hath depth and bulk. Some are so close and reserved, as they will not show their wares but by a dark light, and seem always to keep back somewhat ; and when they know within themselves they speak of that they do not well know, would nevertheless seem to others to know of that which they may not well speak.

Some help themselves with countenance and gesture, and are wise by signs; as Cicero saith of Piso, that when he answered him he fetched one of his brows up to his forehead, and bent the other down to his chin; "Respondes, altero ad frontem sublato, altero ad mentum depresso supercilio, crudelitatem tibi non placere." Some think to bear it by speaking a great word, and being peremptory; and go on, and take by admittance that which they cannot make good. Some, whatsoever is beyond their reach, will seem to despise, or make light of it, as impertinent or curious, and so would have their ignorance seem judgment. Some are never without a difference, and commonly by amusing men with a subtlety, blanch the matter; of whom A. Gellius saith, "Hominem delirum, qui verborum minutiis rerum frangit pondera." Of which kind also Plato, in his *Protagoras*, bringeth in Prodicus in scorn, and maketh him make a speech that consisteth of distinctions from the beginning to the end. Generally, such men, in all deliberations, find ease to be of the negative side, and affect a credit to object and foretell difficulties; for when propositions are denied, there is an end of them; but if they be allowed, it requireth a new work; which false point of wisdom is the bane of business. To conclude, there is no decaying merchant, or

5

inward beggar, hath so many tricks to uphold the credit of their wealth, as these empty persons have to maintain the credit of their sufficiency. Seeming wise men may make shift to get opinion ; but let no man chuse them for employment ; for, certainly, you were better take for business a man somewhat absurd than over-formal.

XXVII

OF FRIENDSHIP

IT had been hard for him that spake it, to have put more truth and untruth together in few words, than in that speech, "Whosoever is delighted in solitude is either a wild beast or a god;" for it is most true, that a natural and secret hatred and aversation towards society, in any man, hath somewhat of the savage beast; but it is most untrue that it should have any character at all of the divine nature, except it proceed, not out of a pleasure in solitude, but out of a love and desire to sequester a man's self for a higher conversation; such as is found to have been falsely and feignedly in some of the heathens—as Epimenides, the Candian; Numa, the Roman; Empedocles, the Sicilian; and Apollonius, of Tyana; and truly, and really, in divers of the ancient hermits and holy fathers of the Church. But little do men perceive what solitude is, and how far it extendeth; for a crowd is not company, and faces are but a gallery of pictures, and talk but a tinkling cymbal, where there is no love. The Latin adage meeteth with it a little : " Magna civitas, magna solitudo,"—because in a great town friends are scattered, so that there is not that fellowship, for the most part, which is in less neighbourhoods ; but we may go farther, and affirm most truly that it is a mere and miserable solitude to want true friends, without which the world is but a wilderness ; and, even in this scene also of solitude, whosoever, in the frame of his nature and affections, is unfit for friendship, he taketh it of the beast, and not from humanity.

A principal fruit of friendship is the ease and discharge of the fullness of the heart, which passions of all kinds do cause and induce. We know diseases of stoppings and suffocations are the most dangerous in the body ; and it is not much otherwise in the mind : you may take sarza to open the liver, steel to open the spleen, flower of sulphur for the lungs, castoreum for the brain ; but no receipt openeth the heart but a true friend, to whom you may impart griefs, joys, fears, hopes, suspicions, counsels, and whatsoever lieth upon the heart to oppress it, in a kind of civil shrift or confession.

It is a strange thing to observe how high a rate great kings and monarchs do set upon this fruit of friendship whereof we speak,—so great, as they purchase it many times at the hazard of their own safety and greatness : for princes, in regard of the distance of their fortune from that of their subjects and servants, cannot gather this fruit, except, to make themselves capable thereof, they raise some persons to be as it were companions, and almost equals to themselves, which many times sorteth to inconvenience. The modern languages give unto such persons the name of favourites, or privadoes,—as if it were matter of grace, or conversation ; but the Roman name attaineth the true use and cause thereof, naming them "participes curarum"; for it is that which tieth the knot : and we see plainly that this hath been done, not by weak and passionate princes only, but by the wisest and most politic that ever reigned, who have oftentimes joined to themselves some of their servants, whom both themselves have called friends, and allowed others likewise to call them in the same manner, using the word which is received between private men.

L. Sylla, when he commanded Rome, raised Pompey, after surnamed The Great, to that height that Pompey vaunted himself for Sylla's over-match ; for when he had carried the consulship for a friend of his, against the pursuit of Sylla, and that Sylla did a little resent thereat, and began to speak great, Pompey turned upon him again, and in effect bade him be quiet; for that more men adored the sun rising than the sun setting. With Julius Cæsar, Decimus Brutus had obtained that interest, as he set him down in his testament for heir in remainder after his nephew; and this was the man that had power with him to draw him forth to his death; for when Cæsar would have discharged the senate, in regard of some ill presages, and especially a dream of Calpurnia, this man lifted him gently by the arm out of his chair, telling him he hoped he would not dismiss the senate till his wife had dreamed a better dream; and it seemed his favour was so great, as Antonius, in a letter, which is recited verbatim in one of Cicero's Philippics, called him "*venefica*," witch, as if he had enchanted Cæsar. Augustus raised Agrippa, though of mean birth, to that height, as, when he consulted with Mæcenas about the marriage of his daughter Julia, Mæcenas took the liberty to tell him that he must either marry his daughter to Agrippa, or take away his life,—there was no third way, he had made him so great. With Tiberius Cæsar, Sejanus had ascended to that height as they two were termed and reckoned as a pair of friends. Tiberius, in a letter to him, saith, "Hæc pro amicitia nostra non occultavi;" and the whole senate dedicated an altar to Friendship, as to a goddess, in respect of the great dearness of friendship between them two. The like, or more, was between Septimus Severus and Plautianus; for he forced his eldest son to marry the daughter of Plautianus, and would often maintain Plautianus in doing affronts to his son; and did write also, in a letter to the senate, by these words, " I love the man so well, as I wish he may over-live me." Now, if these princes had been as a Trajan, or a Marcus Aurelius, a man might have thought that this had proceeded of an abundant goodness of nature: but being men so wise, of such strength and severity of mind, and so extreme lovers of themselves, as all these were, it proveth, most plainly, that they found their own felicity, though as great as ever happened to mortal men, but as a half piece, except they might have a friend to make it entire; and yet, which is more, they were princes that had wives, sons, nephews, yet all these could not supply the comfort of friendship.

It is not to be forgotten what Comineus observeth of his first master, Duke Charles the Hardy—namely, that he would communicate his secrets with none; and, least of all, those secrets which troubled him most. Whereupon he goeth on, and saith, that towards his latter time, that closeness did impair and a little perish his understanding. Surely Comineus might have made the same judgment also, if it had pleased him, of his second master, Louis XI., whose closeness was indeed his tormentor. The parable of Pythagoras is dark, but true, " Cor ne edito "—eat not the heart. Certainly, if a man would give it a hard phrase, those that want friends to open themselves unto are cannibals of their own hearts ; but one thing is most admirable (wherewith I will conclude this first fruit of friendship), which is, that this communicating of a man's self to his friend works to contrary effects, for it re-doubleth joys, and cutteth griefs in halfs ; for there is no man that imparteth his joys to his friend, but he joyeth the more, and no man that imparteth his griefs to his friend, but he grieveth the less. So that it is, in truth, of operations upon a man's mind of like virtue as the alchymists use to attribute to their stone for man's body, that it worketh all contrary effects, but still to the good and benefit of nature. But yet, without praying in aid of alchymists, there is a manifest image of this in the ordinary course of nature ; for, in bodies, union strengtheneth and cherisheth any natural action, and, on the other side, weakeneth and dulleth any violent impression—and even so is it of minds.

The second fruit of friendship is healthful and sovereign for the understanding, as the first is for the affections ; for friendship maketh indeed a fair day in the affections from storm and tempests, but it maketh daylight in the understanding, out of darkness and confusion of thoughts. Neither is this to be understood only of faithful counsel, which a man receiveth from his friend ; but before you come to that, certain it is, that whosoever hath his mind fraught with many thoughts, his wits and understanding do clarify and break up, in the communicating and discoursing with another ; he tosseth his thoughts more easily—he marshalleth them more orderly—he seeth how they look when they are turned into words— finally, he waxeth wiser than himself ; and that more by an hour's discourse than by a day's meditation. It was well said by Themistocles to the king of Persia, " That speech was like cloth of Arras, opened and put abroad "— whereby the imagery doth appear in figure, whereas in thoughts they lie but as in packs. Neither is this second fruit of friendship, in opening the understanding, restrained only to such friends as are able to give a man counsel (they indeed are best), but even without that a man learneth of himself, and bringeth his own thoughts to light, and whetteth his wits as against a stone, which itself cuts not. In a word, a man were better relate himself to a statue or picture, than to suffer his thoughts to pass in smother.

Add now, to make this second fruit of friendship complete, that other point which lieth more open, and falleth within vulgar observation—which is faithful counsel from a friend. Heraclitus saith well, in one of his enigmas, "Dry light is ever the best"; and certain it is, that the light that a man receiveth by counsel from another is drier and purer than that which cometh from his own understanding and judgment, which is ever infused and drenched in his affections and customs. So as there is as much difference between the counsel that a friend giveth, and that a man giveth himself, as there is between the counsel of a friend and of a flatterer; for there is no such flatterer as is a man's self, and there is no such remedy against flattery of a man's self as the liberty of a friend. Counsel is of two sorts; the one concerning manners, the other concerning business: for the first, the best preservative to keep the mind in health is the faithful admonition of a friend. The calling of a man's self to a strict account is a medicine sometimes too piercing and corrosive; reading good books of morality is a little flat and dead; observing our faults in others is sometimes improper for our case; but the best receipt (best, I say, to work, and best to take) is the admonition of a friend. It is a strange thing to behold what gross errors and extreme absurdities many (especially of the greater sort) do commit, for want of a friend to tell them of them, to the great damage both of their fame and fortune : for, as St. James saith, they are as men " that look sometimes into a glass, and presently forget their own shape and favour." As for business, a man may think, if he will, that two eyes see no more than one ; or, that a gamester seeth always more than a looker-on ; or, that a man in anger is as wise as he that hath said over the four-and-twenty letters ; or, that a musket may be shot off as well upon the arm as upon a rest ; and such other fond and high imaginations, to think himself all in all : but when all is done, the help of good counsel is that which setteth business straight ; and if any man think that he will take counsel, but it shall be by pieces ; asking counsel in one business of one man, and in another business of another man ; it is as well (that is to say, better, perhaps, than if he asked none at all), but he runneth two dangers ; one, that he shall not be faithfully counselled— for it is a rare thing, except it be from a perfect and entire friend, to have counsel given, but such as shall be bowed and crooked to some ends which he hath that giveth it ; the other, that he shall have counsel given, hurtful and unsafe (though with good meaning), and mixed partly of mischief and partly of remedy—even as if you would call a physician, that is thought good for the cure of the disease you complain of, but is unacquainted with your body,—and therefore may put you in a way for present cure, but overthroweth your health in some other kind, and so cure the disease, and kill the patient : but a friend, that is wholly acquainted with a man's estate, will beware, by furthering any present business, how he dasheth upon other inconvenience,—and, therefore, rest not upon scattered counsels, for they will rather distract and mislead than settle and direct.

After these two noble fruits of friendship (peace in the affections and support of the judgment) followeth the last fruit, which is, like the pomegranate, full of many kernels—I mean, aid and bearing a part in all actions and occasions. Here, the best way to represent to life the manifold use of friendship is to cast and see how many things there are which a man cannot do himself ; and then it will appear that it was a sparing speech of the ancients, to say " that a friend is another himself," for that a friend is far more than himself. Men have their time, and die many times in desire of some things which they principally take to heart ; the bestowing of a child, the finishing of a work, or the like. If a man have a true friend, he may rest almost secure that the care of those things will continue after him ; so that a man hath, as it were, two lives in his desires.

A man hath a body, and that body is confined to a place ; but where friendship is, all offices of life are, as it were, granted to him and his deputy ; for he may exercise them by his friend. How many things are there which a man cannot, with any face or comeliness say or do himself ? A man can scarce allege his own merits with modesty, much less extol them ; a man cannot sometimes brook to supplicate or beg, and a number of the like : but all these things are graceful in a friend's mouth, which are blushing in a man's own. So, again, a man's person hath many proper relations which he cannot put off. A man cannot speak to his son but as a father ; to his wife but as a husband ; to his enemy but upon terms : whereas a friend may speak as the case requires, and not as it sorteth with the person. But to enumerate these things were endless : I have given the rule, where a man cannot fitly play his own part : if he have not a friend, he may quit the stage.

XXVIII

OF EXPENSE

RICHES are for spending, and spending for honour and good actions—therefore extraordinary expense must be limited by the worth of the occasion : for voluntary undoing may be as well for a man's country as for the kingdom of heaven ; but ordinary expense ought to be limited by a man's estate, and governed with such regard as it be within his compass ; and not subject to deceit and abuse of servants ; and ordered to the best show, that the bills may be less than the estimation abroad. Certainly, if a man will keep but of even hand, his ordinary expenses ought to be but to the half of his receipts ; and if he think to wax rich, but to the third part. It is no baseness for the greatest to descend and look into their own estate. Some forbear it, not upon negligence alone, but doubting to bring themselves into melancholy, in respect they shall find it broken : but wounds cannot be cured without searching.

He that cannot look into his own estate at all had need both chuse well those whom he employeth, and change them often ; for new are more timorous and less subtle. He that can look into his estate but seldom, it behoveth him to turn all to certainties. A man had need, if he be plentiful in some kind of expense, to be as saving again in some other : as, if he be plentiful in diet, to be saving in apparel ; if he be plentiful in the hall, to be saving in the stable, and the like ; for he that is plentiful in expenses of all kinds will hardly be preserved from decay. In clearing of a man's estate, he may as well hurt himself in being too sudden as in letting it run on too long, for hasty selling is commonly as disadvantageable as interest. Besides, he that clears at once will relapse, for, finding himself out of straits, he will revert to his customs ; but he that cleareth by degrees induceth a habit of frugality, and gaineth as well upon his mind as upon his estate. Certainly, who hath a state to repair may not despise small things : and, commonly, it is less dishonourable to abridge petty charges than to stoop to petty gettings. A man ought warily to begin charges which, once begun, will continue ; but in matters that return not, he may be more magnificent.

XXIX

OF THE TRUE GREATNESS OF KINGDOMS AND ESTATES

THE speech of Themistocles, the Athenian, which was haughty and arrogant, in taking so much to himself, had been a grave and wise observation and censure, applied at large to others. Desired at a feast to touch a lute, he said " he could not fiddle, but yet he could make a small town a great city." These words (holpen a little with a metaphor) may express two differing abilities in those that deal in business of estate ; for, if a true survey be taken of counsellors and statesmen, there may be found (though rarely) those which can make a small State great, and yet cannot fiddle,—as, on the other side, there will be found a great many that can fiddle very cunningly, but yet are so far from being able to make a small State great, as their gift lieth the other way—to bring a great and flourishing estate to ruin and decay. And, certainly, those degenerate arts and shifts, whereby many counsellors and governors gain both favour with their masters and estimation with the vulgar, deserve no better name than fiddling, being things rather pleasing for the time, and graceful to themselves only, than tending to the weal and advancement of the State which they serve. There are also (no doubt) counsellors and governors which may be held sufficient, *negotiis pares* [able to manage affairs], and to keep them from precipices and manifest inconveniences, which, nevertheless, are far from the ability to raise and amplify an estate in power, means, and fortune. But be the workmen what they may be, let us speak of the work—that is, the true greatness of kingdoms and estates, and the means thereof. An argument fit for great and mighty princes to have in their hand ; to the end that neither by over-measuring their forces, they lose themselves in vain enterprises ; nor, on the other side, by undervaluing them, they descend to fearful and pusillanimous counsels.

The greatness of an estate, in bulk and territory, doth fall under measure ; and the greatness of finances and revenue doth fall under computation. The population may appear by musters, and the number and greatness of cities and towns by cards and maps ; but yet there is not any thing, amongst civil affairs, more subject to error than the right valuation and true judgment concerning the power and forces of an estate. The kingdom of heaven is compared, not to any great kernel, or nut, but to a grain of mustard-seed; which is one of the least grains, but hath in it a property and spirit hastily to get up and spread. So are there States great in territory, and yet not apt to enlarge or command: and some that have but a small dimension of stem, and yet are apt to be the foundation of great monarchies.

Walled towns, stored arsenals and armories, goodly races of horse, chariots of war, elephants, ordnance, artillery, and the like—all this is but a sheep in a lion's skin, except the breed and disposition of the people be stout and warlike.

Nay, number (itself) in armies importeth not much, where the people are of weak courage; for, as Virgil saith, " It never troubles the wolf how many the sheep be." The army of the Persians, in the plains of Arbela, was such a vast sea of people, as it did somewhat astonish the commanders in Alexander's army, who came to him, therefore, and wished him to set upon them by night; but he answered, " He would not pilfer the victory "—and the defeat was easy. When Tigranes, the Armenian, being encamped upon a hill with four hundred thousand men, discovered the army of the Romans, being not above fourteen thousand, marching towards him, he made himself merry with it, and said, " Yonder men are too many for an ambassage, and too few for a fight ; " but before the sunset, he found them enow to give him the chase with infinite slaughter. Many are the examples of the great odds between number and courage ; so that a man may truly make a judgment, that the principal point of greatness, in any State, is to have a race of military men. Neither is money the sinews of war (as it is trivially said), where the sinews of men's arms in base and effeminate people are failing ; for Solon said well to Crœsus (when in ostentation he showed him his gold), " Sir, if any other come that hath better iron than you, he will be master of all this gold." Therefore, let any prince, or State, think soberly of his forces, except his militia of natives be of good and valiant soldiers ; and let princes, on the other side, that have subjects of martial disposition know their own strength, unless they be otherwise wanting unto themselves. As for mercenary forces (which is the help in this case), all examples show that, whatsoever estate or prince doth rest upon them, he may spread his feathers for a time, but he will mew them soon after.

The blessing of Judah and Issachar will never meet ; that the same people, or nation, should be both the lion's whelp, and the ass between burdens,—neither will it be, that a people overlaid with taxes should ever become valiant and martial. It is true that taxes, levied by consent of the estate, do abate men's courage less, as it hath been seen notably in the excises of the Low Countries, and, in some degree, in the subsidies of England ; for, you must note, that we speak now of the heart, and not of the purse—so that although the same tribute and tax, laid by consent, or by imposing, be all one to the purse, yet it works diversely upon the courage, So that you may conclude that no people overcharged with tribute is fit for empire.

Let States, that aim at greatness, take heed how their nobility and gentlemen do multiply too fast ; for that maketh the common subject grow to be a peasant and base swain, driven out of heart, and, in effect, but a gentleman's labourer. Even as you may see in coppice woods, if you leave your staddles too thick, you shall never have clean underwood, but shrubs and bushes ; so in countries, if the gentlemen be too many, the commons will be base—and you will bring it to that, that not the hundredth poll will be fit for an helmet, especially as to the infantry, which is the nerve of an army,—and so there will be great population and little strength. This which I speak of hath been nowhere better seen than by comparing of England and France; whereof England, though far less in territory and population, hath been, nevertheless, an overmatch; in regard the middle people of England make good soldiers, which the peasants of France do not: herein the device of King Henry VII. (whereof I have spoken largely in the history of his life) was profound and admirable, in making farms and houses of husbandry of a standard, that is, maintained with such a proportion of land unto them, as may breed a subject to live in convenient plenty, and no servile condition; and to keep the plough in the hands of the owners, and not mere hirelings; and thus indeed you shall attain to Virgil's character, which he gives to ancient Italy:—

"Terra potens armis atque ubere glebæ."

Neither is the estate (which for anything I know is almost peculiar to England, and hardly to be found anywhere else, except it be, perhaps, in Poland) to be passed over—I mean the state of free servants and attendants upon noblemen and gentlemen, which are no ways inferior unto the yeomanry for arms; and therefore, out of all question, the splendour and magnificence and great retinues, the hospitality of noblemen and gentlemen received into custom, do much conduce unto martial greatness—whereas, contrariwise, the close and reserved living of noblemen and gentlemen causeth a penury of military forces.

By all means it is to be procured, that the trunk of Nebuchadnezzar's tree of monarchy be great enough to bear the branches and the boughs ; that is, that the natural subjects of the crown, or State, bear a sufficient proportion to the strange subjects that they govern. Therefore all States that are liberal of naturalization towards strangers are fit for empire ; for to think that an handful of people can, with the greatest courage and policy in the world, embrace too large extent of dominion, it may hold for a time, but it will fail suddenly. The Spartans were a nice people in point of naturalization ; whereby, while they kept their compass, they stood firm, but when they did spread, and their boughs were become too great for their stem, they became a windfall upon the sudden. Never any State was, in this point, so open to receive strangers into their Body as were the Romans ; therefore it sorted with them accordingly, for they grew to the greatest monarchy. Their manner was to grant naturalization (which they called " jus civitatis ")— and to grant it in the highest degree, that is, not only " jus commercii, jus connubii, jus hæreditatis," but also " jus suffragii " and " jus honorum " ; and this not to singular persons alone, but likewise to whole families—yea, to cities, and sometimes to nations. Add to this their custom of plantation of colonies, whereby the Roman plant was removed into the soil of other nations ; and, putting both constitutions together, you will say that it was not the Romans that spread upon the world, but it was the world that spread upon the Romans—and that was the sure way of greatness. I have marvelled sometimes at Spain, how they clasp and contain so large dominions with so few natural Spaniards : but sure the whole compass of Spain is a very great body of a tree, far above Rome and Sparta at the first ; and, besides, though they have not had that usage to naturalize liberally, yet they have that which is next to it—that is, to employ, almost indifferently, all nations in their militia of ordinary soldiers, yea, and sometimes in their highest commands ; nay, it seemeth at this instant, they are sensible of this want of natives, as by the Pragmatical Sanction, now published, appeareth.

It is certain, that sedentary and within-door arts, and delicate manufactures (that require rather the finger than the arm), have in their nature a contrariety to a military disposition ; and generally all warlike people are a little idle, and love danger better than travail—neither must they be too much broken off it, if they shall be preserved in vigour : therefore it was great advantage in the ancient states of Sparta, Athens, Rome, and others, that they had the use of slaves, which commonly did rid those manufactures ; but that is abolished, in greatest part, by the Christian law. That which cometh nearest to it is to leave those arts chiefly to strangers (which, for that purpose, are the more easily to be received), and to contain the principal bulk of the vulgar natives within those three kinds—tillers of the ground, free servants, and handicraftsmen of strong and manly arts, as smiths, masons, carpenters, &c., not reckoning professed soldiers.

But, above all, for empire and greatness, it importeth most that a nation do profess arms as their principal honour, study, and occupation ; for the things which we have formerly spoken of are but habilitations towards arms ; and what is habilitation without intention and act ? Romulus, after his death (as they report, or feign), sent a present to the Romans, that above all they should intend arms, and then they should prove the greatest empire of the world. The fabric of the State of Sparta was wholly (though not wisely) framed and composed to that scope and end : the Persians and Macedonians had it for a flash ; the Gauls, Germans, Goths, Saxons, Normans, and others, had it for a time ; the Turks have it at this day, though in great declination. Of Christian Europe, they that have it are, in effect, only the Spaniards; but it is so plain, that every man profiteth in that he most intendeth, that it needeth not to be stood upon; it is enough to point at it—that no nation which doth not directly profess arms may look to have greatness fall into their mouths: and, on the other side, it is a most certain oracle of time, that those States that continue long in that profession (as the Romans and Turks principally have done) do wonders; and those that have professed arms but for an age have, notwithstanding, commonly attained that greatness in that age which maintained them long after, when their profession and exercise of arms hath grown to decay.

Incident to this point is for a State to have those laws or customs which may reach forth unto them just occasions (as may be pretended) of war; for there is that justice imprinted in the nature of men, that they enter not upon wars (whereof so many calamities do ensue), but upon some, at the least specious, grounds and quarrels. The Turk hath at hand, for cause of war, the propagation of his law or sect, a quarrel that he may always command. The Romans, though they esteemed the extending the limits of their empire to be great honour to their generals when it was done, yet they never rested upon that alone to begin a war. First, therefore, let nations that pretend to greatness have this, that they be sensible of wrongs, either upon borderers, merchants, or politic ministers; and that they sit not too long upon a provocation: secondly, let them be prest and ready to give aids and succours to their confederates, as it ever was with the Romans; insomuch, as if the confederates had leagues defensive with divers other States, and, upon invasion offered, did implore their aids severally, yet the Romans would ever be the foremost, and leave it to none other to have the honour. As for the wars which were anciently made on the behalf of a kind of party, or tacit conformity of state, I do not see how they may be well justified; as when the Romans made a war for the liberty of Græcia, or when the Lacedæmonians and Athenians made war to set up or pull down democracies and oligarchies; or when wars were made by foreigners, under the pretence of justice or protection, to deliver the subjects of others from tyranny and oppression, and the like. Let it suffice, that no estate expect to be great that is not awake upon any just occasion of arming.

No body can be healthful without exercise, neither natural body nor politic; and certainly, to a kingdom or estate, a just and honourable war is the true exercise. A civil war, indeed, is like the heat of a fever ; but a foreign war is like the heat of exercise, and serveth to keep the body in health ; for in a slothful peace, both courages will effeminate, and manners corrupt : but howsoever it be for happiness, without all question for greatness, it maketh to be still for the most part in arms : and the strength of a veteran army (though it be a chargeable business), always on foot, is that which commonly giveth the law, or, at least, the reputation amongst all neighbour States, as may be well seen in Spain ; which hath had, in one part or other, a veteran army almost continually, now by the space of six-score years.

To be master of the sea is an abridgment of a monarchy. Cicero, writing to Atticus of Pompey's preparation against Cæsar, saith, " Concilium Pompeii plane Themistocleum est ; putat enim, qui mari potitur, eum rerum potiri ; " and without doubt, Pompey had tired out Cæsar, if upon vain confidence he had not left that way. We see the great effects of battles by sea : the battle of Actium decided the empire of the world ; the battle of Lepanto arrested the greatness of the Turk. There be many examples where sea-fights have been final to the war ; but this is when Princes, or States, have set up their rest upon the battles ; but thus much is certain, that he that commands the sea is at great liberty, and may take as much and as little of the war as he will ; whereas those that be strongest by land are many times, nevertheless, in great straits. Surely, at this day, with us of Europe, the vantage of strength at sea (which is one of the principal dowries of this kingdom of Great Britain) is great ; both because most of the kingdoms of Europe are not merely inland, but girt with the sea most part of their compass, and because the wealth of both Indies seems, in great part, but an accessory to the command of the seas.

The wars of later ages seem to be made in the dark, in respect of the glory and honour which reflected upon men from the wars in ancient time. There be now, for martial encouragement, some degrees and orders of chivalry, which, nevertheless, are conferred promiscuously upon soldiers and no soldiers, and some remembrance perhaps upon the escutcheon, and some hospitals for maimed soldiers, and suchlike things ; but in ancient times, the trophies erected upon the place of the victory, the funeral laudatives and monuments for those that died in the wars, the crowns and garlands personal, the style of emperor, which the great kings of the world after borrowed, the triumphs of the generals upon their return, the great donatives and

largesses upon the disbanding of the armies,
were things able to inflame all men's courages ;
but, above all, that of the triumph amongst the
Romans was not pageants, or gaudery, but one
of the wisest and noblest institutions that ever
was : for it contained three things, honour to
the general, riches to the treasury out of the
spoils, and donatives to the army : but that
honour, perhaps, were not fit for monarchies,
except it be in the person of the monarch himself, or his sons ; as it came to pass in the times
of the Roman emperors, who did impropriate
the actual triumphs to themselves and their
sons, for such wars as they did achieve in
person, and left only for wars achieved by
subjects some triumphal garments and ensigns
to the general.

To conclude. No man can by care-taking
(as the Scripture saith) " add a cubit to his
stature," in this little model of a man's body ;
but in the great fame of kingdoms and commonwealths, it is in the power of princes, or
estates, to add amplitude and greatness to their
kingdoms ; for by introducing such ordinances,
constitutions, and customs, as we have now
touched, they may sow greatness to their
posterity and succession. But these things are
commonly not observed, but left to take their
chance.

XXX

OF REGIMEN OF HEALTH

THERE is a wisdom in this beyond the rules of physic : a man's own observation, what he finds good of, and what he finds hurt of, is the best physic to preserve health ; but it is a safer conclusion to say, " This agreeth not well with me, therefore I will not continue it," than this, " I find no offence of this, therefore I may use it : " for strength of nature in youth passeth over many excesses which are owing a man till his age. Discern of the coming on of years, and think not to do the same things still ; for age will not be defied. Beware of sudden change in any great point of diet, and if necessity enforce it, fit the rest to it ; for it is a secret, both in nature and state, that it is safer to change many things than one. Examine thy customs of diet, sleep, exercise, apparel, and the like, and try, in anything thou shalt judge hurtful, to discontinue it by little and little ; but so as if thou dost find any inconvenience by the change, thou come back to it again; for it is hard to distinguish that which is generally held good and wholesome, from that which is good particularly, and fit for thine own body. To be free-minded and cheerfully disposed at hours of meat and sleep, and of exercise, is one of the best precepts of long lasting. As for the passions and studies of the mind, avoid envy, anxious fears, anger, fretting inwards, subtle and knotty inquisitions, joys and exhilarations in excess, sadness not communicated. Entertain hopes, mirth rather than joy, variety of delights rather than surfeit of them; wonder and admiration, and therefore novelties; studies that fill the mind with splendid and illustrious objects, as histories, fables, and contemplations of nature. If you fly physic in health altogether, it will be too strange for your body when you shall need it; if you make it too familiar, it will work no extraordinary effect when sickness cometh. I commend rather some diet for certain seasons, than frequent use of physic, except it be grown into a custom; for those diets alter the body more, and trouble it less. Despise no new accident in your body, but ask opinion of it. In sickness, respect health principally, and in health, action; for those that put their bodies to endure in health may in most sicknesses which are not very sharp be cured only with diet and tendering.

Celsus could never have spoken it as a physician, had he not been a wise man withal, when he giveth it for one of the great precepts of health and lasting, that a man do vary and interchange contraries, but with an inclination to the more benign extreme ; use fasting and full eating, but rather full eating ; watching and sleep, but rather sleep ; sitting and exercise, but rather exercise, and the like ; so shall nature be cherished and yet taught masteries. Physicians are some of them so pleasing and conformable to the humour of the patient, as they press not the true cure of the disease ; and some others are so regular in proceeding according to art for the disease, as they respect not sufficiently the condition of the patient. Take one of a middle temper, or, if it may not be found in one man, combine two of either sort ; and forget not to call as well the best acquainted with your body, as the best reputed of for his faculty.

XXXI

OF SUSPICION

SUSPICIONS amongst thoughts are like bats amongst birds,—they ever fly by twilight ; certainly they are to be repressed, or, at the least, well guarded, for they cloud the mind, they lose friends, and they check with business, whereby business cannot go on currently and constantly ; they dispose kings to tyranny, husbands to jealousy, wise men to irresolution and melancholy ; they are defects, not in the heart, but in the brain, for they take place in the stoutest natures, as in the example of Henry VII. of England. There was not a more suspicious man nor a more stout ; and in such a composition they do small hurt, for commonly they are not admitted but with examination whether they be likely or no ; but in fearful natures they gain ground too fast. There is nothing makes a man suspect much, more than to know little ; and, therefore, men should remedy suspicion by procuring to know

6

more, and not to keep their suspicions in smother. What would men have?—do they think those they employ and deal with are saints? do they not think they will have their own ends, and be truer to themselves than to them? therefore there is no better way to moderate suspicions than to account upon such suspicions as true, and yet to bridle them as false: for so far a man ought to make use of suspicions as to provide, as if that should be true that he suspects, yet it may do him no hurt. Suspicions that the mind of itself gathers are but buzzes; but suspicions that are artificially nourished, and put into men's heads by the tales and whisperings of others, have stings. Certainly, the best mean to clear the way in this same wood of suspicion is frankly to communicate them with the party that he suspects: for thereby he shall be sure to know more of the truth of them than he did before, and withal shall make that party more circumspect, not to give further cause of suspicion; but this would not be done to men of base natures, for they, if they find themselves once suspected, will never be true. The Italian says, " Sospetto licentia fede ; " as if suspicion did give a passport to faith; but it ought rather to kindle it to discharge itself.

XXXII

OF DISCOURSE

SOME in their discourse desire rather commendation of wit, in being able to hold all arguments, than of judgment, in discerning what is true ; as if it were a praise to know what might be said, and not what should be thought. Some have certain commonplaces and themes, wherein they are good, and want variety ; which kind of poverty is for the most part tedious, and, when it is once perceived, ridiculous. The honourablest part of the talk is to give the occasion ; and again to moderate and pass to somewhat else, for then a man leads the dance. It is good in discourse, and speech of conversation, to vary and intermingle speech of the present occasion with arguments, tales with reason, asking of questions with telling of opinions, and jest with earnest ; for it is a dull thing to tire, and as we say now to jade anything too far. As for jest, there be certain things which ought to be privileged from it—namely, religion, matters of state, great persons,

any man's present business of importance, and
any case that deserveth pity ; yet there be
some that think their wits have been asleep,
except they dart out somewhat that is piquant,
and to the quick—that is a vein which would
be bridled :—

" Parce puer stimulis, et fortius utere loris."

And, generally, men ought to find the difference between saltness and bitterness. Certainly, he that hath a satirical vein, as he maketh
others afraid of his wit, so he had need be
afraid of others' memory. He that questioneth
much shall learn much, and content much, but
especially if he apply his questions to the skill
of the persons whom he asketh, for he shall
give them occasion to please themselves in
speaking, and himself shall continually gather
knowledge ; but let his questions not be troublesome, for that is fit for a poser ; and let him be
sure to leave other men their turns to speak—
nay, if there be any that would reign and take
up all the time, let him find means to take
them off and bring others on, as musicians use
to do with those that dance too long galliards.
If you dissemble sometimes your knowledge
of that you are thought to know, you shall
be thought, another time, to know that you
know not. Speech of a man's self ought to
be seldom, and well chosen. I knew one was

wont to say in scorn, " He must needs be a wise man, he speaks so much of himself,"—and there is but one case wherein a man may commend himself with a good grace, and that is in commending virtue in another, especially if it be such a virtue whereunto himself pretendeth. Speech of touch towards others should be sparingly used ; for discourse ought to be as a field, without coming home to any man. I knew two noblemen, of the west part of England, whereof the one was given to scoff, but kept ever royal cheer in his house ; the other would ask of those that had been at the other's table, " Tell truly, was there never a flout or dry blow given ? " To which the guest would answer, " Such and such a thing passed." The lord would say, " I thought he would mar a good dinner." Discretion of speech is more than eloquence ; and to speak agreeably to him with whom we deal is more than to speak in good words or in good order. A good continued speech, without a good speech of interlocution, shows slowness ; and a good reply, or second speech, without a good settled speech, showeth shallowness and weakness. As we see in beasts, that those that are weakest in the course are yet nimblest in the turn ; as it is betwixt the greyhound and the hare. To use too many circumstances ere one come to the matter is wearisome ; to use none at all is blunt.

XXXIII

OF PLANTATIONS

PLANTATIONS are amongst ancient, primitive, and heroical works. When the world was young it begat more children, but now it is old, it begets fewer ; for I may justly account new plantations to be the children of former kingdoms. I like a plantation in a pure soil, that is, where people are not displanted to the end to plant in others ; for else it is rather an extirpation than a plantation. Planting of countries is like planting of woods ; for you must make account to lose almost twenty years' profit, and expect your recompense in the end ; for the principal thing that hath been the destruction of most plantations hath been the base and hasty drawing of profit in the first years. It is true, speedy profit is not to be neglected, as far as it may stand with the good of the plantation, but no farther.

It is a shameful and unblessed thing to take the scum of people and wicked condemned men, to be the people with whom you plant; and not only so, but it spoileth the plantation; for they will ever live like rogues, and not fall to work, but be lazy, and do mischief, and spend victuals, and be quickly weary, and then certify over to their country to the discredit of the plantation. The people wherewith you plant ought to be gardeners, ploughmen, labourers, smiths, carpenters, joiners, fishermen, fowlers, with some few apothecaries, surgeons, cooks, and bakers. In a country of plantation, first look about what kind of victual the country yields of itself to hand; as chesnuts, walnuts, pine-apples, olives, dates, plums, cherries, wild honey, and the like, and make use of them. Then consider what victual or esculent things there are, which grow speedily, and within the year; as parsneps, carrots, turnips, onions, radish, artichokes of Jerusalem, maize, and the like: for wheat, barley, and oats, they ask too much labour; but with peas and beans you may begin, both because they ask less labour, and because they serve for meat as well as for bread; and of rice likewise cometh a great increase, and it is a kind of meat. Above all, there ought to be brought store of biscuit, oatmeal, flour, meal, and the like, in the beginning, till bread may be had. For beasts or birds, take chiefly such as are least subject to diseases, and multiply fastest: as swine, goats, cocks, hens, turkeys, geese, house-doves, and the like. The victual in plantations ought to be expended almost as in a besieged town, that is, with certain allowance; and let the main part of the ground employed to gardens or corn be to a common stock, and to be laid in, and stored up, and then delivered out in proportion; besides some spots of ground that any particular person will manure for his own private. Consider likewise, what commodities the soil where the plantation is doth naturally yield, that they may some way help to defray the charge of the plantation; so it be not, as was said, to the untimely prejudice of the main business, as it hath fared with tobacco in Virginia. Wood commonly aboundeth but too much, and therefore timber is fit to be one. If there be iron ore, and streams whereupon to set the mills, iron is a brave commodity where wood aboundeth. Making of bay salt, if the climate be proper for it, would be put in experience; growing silk, likewise, if any be, is a likely commodity; pitch and tar, where store of firs and pines are, will not fail; so drugs and sweet woods, where they are, cannot but yield great profit; soap ashes likewise, and other things that may be thought of; but moil not too much under ground, for the hope of mines is very uncertain, and useth to make the planters lazy in other things. For government, let it be in the hands of one, assisted with some counsel, and let them have commission to exercise martial laws, with some limitation. And, above all, let men make that profit of being in the wilderness, as they have God always, and his service before their eyes. Let not the government of the plantation depend upon too many counsellors and undertakers in the country that planteth, but upon a temperate number; and let those be rather noblemen and gentlemen, than merchants; for they look ever to the present gain. Let there be freedoms from custom, till the plantation be of strength, and not only freedom from custom, but freedom to carry their commodities where they may make their best of them, except there be some special cause of caution. Cram not in people, by sending too fast, company after company, but rather hearken how they waste, and send supplies proportionably; but so as the number may live well in the plantation, and not by surcharge be in penury. It hath been a great endangering to the health of some plantations, that they have built along the sea and rivers, in marish and unwholesome grounds; therefore, though you begin there, to avoid carriage and other like discommodities, yet build still rather upwards from the stream, than along it. It concerneth likewise the health of the plantation that they have good store of salt with them, that they may use it in their victuals when it shall be necessary.

If you plant where savages are, do not only entertain them with trifles and gingles, but use them justly and graciously, with sufficient guard, nevertheless ; and do not win their favour by helping them to invade their enemies, but for their defence, it is not amiss ; and send oft of them over to the country that plants, that they may see a better condition than their own, and commend it when they return.

When the plantation grows to strength, then it is time to plant with women as well as with men, that the plantation may spread into generations, and not be ever pieced from without. It is the sinfullest thing in the world to forsake or destitute a plantation once in forwardness ; for, besides the dishonour, it is the guiltiness of blood of many commiserable persons.

XXXIV

OF RICHES

I CANNOT call riches better than the baggage of virtue ; the Roman word is better—*impedimenta* ; for as the baggage is to an army, so is riches to virtue—it cannot be spared nor left behind, but it hindereth the march ; yea, and the care of it sometimes loseth or disturbeth the victory. Of great riches there is no real use, except it be in the distribution ; the rest is but conceit ; so saith Solomon, " Where much is, there are many to consume it ; and what hath the owner but the sight of it with his eyes ? " The personal fruition in any man cannot reach to feel great riches : there is a custody of them, or a power of dole, and a donative of them, or a fame of them, but no solid use to the owner. Do you not see what feigned prices are set upon little stones and rarities—and what works of ostentation are undertaken, because there might seem to be some use of great riches ? But then, you will

say, they may be of use to buy men out of
dangers or troubles ; as Solomon saith, " Riches
are as a stronghold in the imagination of the
rich man : " but this is excellently expressed,
that it is in imagination, and not always in
fact ; for, certainly great riches have sold more
men than they have bought out. Seek not
proud riches, but such as thou mayest get
justly, use soberly, distribute cheerfully, and
leave contentedly ; yet have no abstract or
friarly contempt of them, but distinguish,
as Cicero saith well of Rabirius Posthumus,
" In studio rei amplificandæ, apparebat, non
avaritiæ prædam, sed instrumentum bonitati
quæri." Hearken also to Solomon, and beware
of hasty gathering of riches : " Qui festinat ad
divitias, non erit insons." The poets feign
that when Plutus (which is riches) is sent from
Jupiter, he limps, and goes slowly, but when
he is sent from Pluto, he runs, and is swift of
foot ; meaning, that riches gotten by good
means and just labour pace slowly, but when
they come by the death of others (as by the
course of inheritance, testaments, and the like),
they come tumbling upon a man : but it might
be applied likewise to Pluto taking him for the
Devil ; for when riches come from the Devil (as
by fraud, and oppression, and unjust means)
they come upon speed. The ways to enrich
are many, and most of them foul : parsimony

is one of the best, and yet is not innocent, for
it withholdeth men from works of liberality
and charity. The improvement of the ground
is the most natural obtaining of riches, for it is
our great mother's blessing, the earth; but it
is slow: and yet, where men of great wealth
do stoop to husbandry, it multiplieth riches
exceedingly. I knew a nobleman of England
that had the greatest audits of any man in my
time,—a great grazier, a great sheep master, a
great timber man, a great collier, a great corn
master, a great lead man, and so of iron, and a
number of the like points of husbandry; so as
the earth seemed a sea to him in respect of the
perpetual importation. It was truly observed
by one, " That himself came very hardly to
little riches, and very easily to great riches; "
for when a man's stock is come to that, that he
can expect the prime of markets, and overcome
those bargains, which for their greatness are
few men's money, and be partner in the industries of younger men, he cannot but increase
mainly. The gains of ordinary trades and
vocations are honest, and furthered by two
things, chiefly, by diligence, and by a good
name for good and fair dealing; but the gains
of bargains are of a more doubtful nature, when
men shall wait upon others' necessity; broke
by servants, and instruments to draw them on;
put off others cunningly that would be better

chapmen, and the like practices, which are crafty and naughty. As for the chopping of bargains, when a man buys not to hold, but to sell over again, that commonly grindeth double, both upon the seller and upon the buyer. Sharings do greatly enrich, if the hands be well chosen that are trusted. Usury is the certainest means of gain, though one of the worst, as that whereby a man doth eat his bread, " *in sudore vultus alieni,*" and besides, doth plough upon Sundays : but yet certain though it be, it hath flaws : for that the scriveners and brokers do value unsound men to serve their own turn. The fortune in being the first in an invention, or in a privilege, doth cause sometimes a wonderful overgrowth in riches ; as it was with the first sugar man in the Canaries : therefore, if a man can play the true logician, to have as well judgment as invention, he may do great matters, especially if the times be fit. He that resteth upon gains certain, shall hardly grow to great riches ; and he that puts all upon adventures, doth oftentimes break and come to poverty : it is good, therefore, to guard adventures with certainties that may uphold losses. Monopolies, and coemption of wares for resale, where they are not restrained, are great means to enrich ; especially if the party have intelligence what things are like to come into request, and so store himself beforehand.

Riches gotten by service, though it be of the best rise, yet when they are gotten by flattery, feeding humours, and other servile conditions, they may be placed among the worst. As for "fishing for testaments and executorships" (as Tacitus saith of Seneca, "Testamenta et orbos tanquam indagine capi"), it is yet worse, by how much men submit themselves to meaner persons than in service.

Believe not much them that seem to despise riches, for they despise them that despair of them; and none worse when they come to them. Be not penny-wise; riches have wings, and sometimes they fly away of themselves, sometimes they must be set flying to bring in more. Men leave their riches either to their kindred, or to the Public; and moderate portions prosper best in both. A great estate left to an heir is as a lure to all the birds of prey round about to seize on him, if he be not the better stablished in years and judgment: likewise, glorious gifts and foundations are like sacrifices without salt; and but the painted sepulchres of alms, which soon will putrefy and corrupt inwardly. Therefore measure not thine advancements by quantity, but frame them by measure: and defer not charities till death: for, certainly, if a man weigh it rightly, he that doth so is rather liberal of another man's than of his own.

XXXV

OF PROPHECIES

I MEAN not to speak of divine prophecies,
nor of heathen oracles, nor of natural predictions, but only of prophecies that have been
of certain memory, and from hidden causes.
Saith the Pythonissa to Saul, " To-morrow
thou and thy sons shall be with me." Virgil
hath these verses from Homer :

" At domus Æneæ cunctis dominabitur oris,
     Et nati natorum, et qui nascentur ab illis : "

a prophecy, as it seems, of the Roman empire.
Seneca the tragedian hath these verses :

                    " Venient annis
        Sæcula seris, quibus Oceanus
        Vincula rerum laxet, et ingens
        Pateat tellus, Tiphysque novos
        Detegat orbes ; nec sit terris
        Ultima Thule : "

a prophecy of the discovery of America. The

daughter of Polycrates dreamed that Jupiter bathed her father, and Apollo anointed him; and it came to pass that he was crucified in an open place, where the sun made his body run with sweat, and the rain washed it. Philip of Macedon dreamed he sealed up his wife's belly; whereby he did expound it, that his wife should be barren; but Aristander, the soothsayer, told him his wife was with child, because men do not use to seal vessels that are empty. A phantom that appeared to M. Brutus in his tent said to him, " Philippis iterum me videbis." Tiberius said to Galba, " Tu quoque, Galba, degustabis imperium." In Vespasian's time there went a prophecy in the East, that those that should come forth of Judea should reign over the world; which, though it may be was meant of our Saviour, yet Tacitus expounds it of Vespasian. Domitian dreamed, the night before he was slain, that a golden head was growing out of the nape of his neck; and, indeed, the succession that followed him, for many years, made golden times. Henry VI. of England said of Henry VII. when he was a lad, and gave him water, " This is the lad that shall enjoy the crown for which we strive." When I was in France, I heard from one Dr. Pena, that the queen-mother, who was given to curious arts, caused the king her husband's nativity to be calculated under a false name, and the astrologer gave a judgment that he should be killed in a duel; at which the queen laughed, thinking her husband to be above challenges and duels; but he was slain upon a course at tilt, the splinters of the staff of Montgomery going in at his beaver. The trivial prophecy which I heard when I was a child, and Queen Elizabeth was in the flower of her years, was,

> " When hempe is spun,
> England's done : "

whereby it was generally conceived, that after the princes had reigned which had the principal letters of that word hempe, which were Henry, Edward, Mary, Philip, and Elizabeth, England should come to utter confusion; which, thanks be to God, is verified in the change of the name, for the king's style is now no more of England, but of Britain. There was also another prophecy before the year of eighty-eight, which I do not well understand :

> " There shall be seen upon a day,
> Between the Baugh and the May,
> The Black fleet of Norway.
> When that is come and gone,
> England build houses of lime and stone,
> For after wars shall you have none."

It was generally conceived to be meant of the Spanish fleet that came in eighty-eight; for that

the King of Spain's surname, as they say, is
Norway.   The prediction of Regiomontanus,

" *Octogesimus octavus mirabilis annus,*"

was thought likewise accomplished in the sending of that great fleet, being the greatest in
strength, though not in number, of all that
ever swam upon the sea.   As for Cleon's dream,
I think it was a jest—it was, that he was de-
voured of a long dragon ; and it was expounded
of a maker of sausages, that troubled him exceedingly.   There are numbers of the like kind,
especially if you include dreams, and predictions
of astrology ; but I have set down these few
only of certain credit, for example.   My judgment is, that they ought all to be despised, and
ought to serve but for winter-talk by the fire-
side.   Though when I say despised, I mean it
as for belief—for otherwise, the spreading or
publishing of them is in no sort to be despised
—for they have done much mischief, and I see
many severe laws made to suppress them.   That
that hath given them grace, and some credit,
consisteth in three things.   First, that men
mark when they hit, and never mark when
they miss ; as they do, generally, also of dreams.
The second is, that probable conjectures, or
obscure traditions, many times turn themselves
into prophecies : while the nature of man which
coveteth divination thinks it no peril to fore-

tell that which indeed they do but collect, as that of Seneca's verse ; for so much was then subject to demonstration, that the globe of the earth had great parts beyond the Atlantic, which might be probably conceived not to be all sea, and adding thereto the tradition in Plato's *Timæus* and his *Atlanticus*, it might encourage one to turn it to a prediction. The third and last, which is the great one, is, that almost all of them, being infinite in number, have been impostures, and by idle and crafty brains, merely contrived and feigned, after the event past.

XXXVI

OF AMBITION

AMBITION is like choler, which is a humour that maketh men active, earnest, full of alacrity, and stirring, if it be not stopped ; but if it be stopped, and cannot have its way, it becometh adust, and thereby malign and venomous ; so ambitious men, if they find the way open for their rising, and still get forward, they are rather busy than dangerous ; but if they be checked in their desires, they become secretly discontent, and look upon men and matters with an evil eye, and are best pleased when things go backward ; which is the worst property in a servant of a prince or State. Therefore, it is good for princes, if they use ambitious men, to handle it so as they be still progressive and not retrograde ; which, because it cannot be without inconvenience, it is good not to use such natures at all ; for if they rise not with their service, they will take order to make their service fall with them. But since we have said it were good not to use men of ambitious natures, except it be upon necessity, it is fit to speak in what cases they are of necessity. Good commanders in the wars must be taken, be they never so ambitious; for the use of their service dispenseth with the rest; and to take a soldier without ambition is to pull off his spurs. There is also great use of ambitious men in being screens to princes in matters of danger and envy; for no man will take that part except he be like a seeled dove, that mounts and mounts, because he cannot see about him. There is use also of ambitious men in pulling down the greatness of any subject that overtops; as Tiberius used Macro in the pulling down of Sejanus. Since, therefore, they must be used in such cases, there resteth to speak how they are to be bridled, that they may be less dangerous. There is less danger of them, if they be of mean birth, than if they be noble; and if they be rather harsh of nature, than gracious and popular, and if they be rather new raised, than grown cunning and fortified in their greatness. It is counted by some a weakness in princes to have favourites, but it is, of all others, the best remedy against ambitious great ones; for when the way of pleasuring and displeasuring lieth by the favourite, it is impossible any other should be over great. Another means to curb them is to balance them by others as proud as they; but then there must be some middle counsellors to keep things steady, for without that ballast the ship will roll too much. At the least, a prince may animate and inure some meaner persons to be scourges to ambitious men. As for the having of them obnoxious to ruin, if they be of fearful natures, it may do well, but if they be stout and daring, it may precipitate their designs, and prove dangerous. As for the pulling of them down, if the affairs require it, and that it may not be done with safety suddenly, the only way is the interchange continually of favours and disgraces, whereby they may not know what to expect, and be, as it were, in a wood. Of ambitions, it is less harmful, the ambition to prevail in great things, than that other to appear in every thing; for that breeds confusion, and mars business; but yet it is less danger to have an ambitious man stirring in business, than great in dependencies. He that seeketh to be eminent amongst able men hath a great task, but that is ever good for the public; but he that plots to be the only figure amongst cyphers is the decay of a whole age. Honour hath three things in it; the vantage ground to do good, the approach to kings and principal persons, and the raising of a man's own fortunes. He that hath the best of these intentions, when he aspireth, is an honest man;

and that prince that can discern of these intentions in another that aspireth is a wise prince. Generally, let princes and States chuse such ministers as are more sensible of duty than of rising, and such as love business rather upon conscience than upon bravery ; and let them discern a busy nature from a willing mind.

XXXVII

OF MASQUES AND TRIUMPHS

THESE things are but toys to come amongst such serious observations ; but yet, since princes will have such things, it is better they should be graced with elegancy than daubed with cost. Dancing to song is a thing of great state and pleasure. I understand it that the song be in quire, placed aloft, and accompanied with some broken music, and the ditty fitted to the device. Acting in song, especially in dialogues, hath an extreme good grace—I say acting, not dancing (for that is a mean and vulgar thing) ; and the voices of the dialogue would be strong and manly (a bass and a tenor, no treble), and the ditty high and tragical, not nice or dainty. Several quires placed one over against another, and taking the voice by catches, anthem-wise, give great pleasure. Turning dances into figure is a childish curiosity ; and generally let it be noted, that those things which I here set down are such as do naturally take the sense, and not respect petty wonderments. It is true, the alterations of scenes, so it be quietly and without noise, are things of great beauty and pleasure ; for they feed and relieve the eye before it be full of the same object. Let the scenes abound with light, especially coloured and varied, and let the masquers, or any other that are to come down from the scene, have some motions upon the scene itself before their coming down ; for it draws the eye strangely, and makes it with great pleasure to desire to see that it cannot perfectly discern. Let the songs be loud and cheerful, and not chirpings or pulings ; let the music likewise be sharp and loud, and well placed. The colours that show best by candle-light are white, carnation, and a kind of sea-water green ; and ouches, or spangs, as they are of no great cost, so they are of most glory. As for rich embroidery, it is lost and not discerned. Let the suits of the masquers be graceful, and such as become the person when the vizards are off, not after examples of known attires, Turks, soldiers, mariners, and the like. Let anti-masques not be long ; they have been commonly of fools, satyrs, baboons, wild men, antics, beasts, sprites, witches, Æthiopes, pigmies, turquets, nymphs, rustics, Cupids, statues moving, and the like. As for angels, it is not comical enough to put them in anti-masques ; and anything that is hideous, as devils, giants, is, on the other side, as unfit ; but chiefly, let the music of them be recreative, and with some strange changes. Some sweet odours suddenly coming forth, without any drops falling, are, in such a company, as there is steam and heat, things of great pleasure and refreshment. Double masques, one of men, another of ladies, addeth state and variety ; but all is nothing except the room be kept clear and neat.

For justs, and tourneys, and barriers, the glories of them are chiefly in the chariots, wherein the challengers make their entry, especially if they be drawn with strange beasts, as lions, bears, camels, and the like ; or, in the devices of their entrance, or in bravery of their liveries, or in the goodly furniture of their horses and armour. But enough of these toys.

XXXVIII

OF NATURE IN MEN

NATURE is often hidden, sometimes overcome, seldom extinguished. Force maketh nature more violent in the return, doctrine and discourse maketh nature less importune, but custom only doth alter and subdue nature. He that seeketh victory over his nature, let him not set himself too great nor too small tasks ; for the first will make him dejected by often failing, and the second will make him a small proceeder, though by often prevailing. And, at the first, let him practise with helps, as swimmers do with bladders or rushes ; but, after a time, let him practise with disadvantages, as dancers do with thick shoes, for it breeds great perfection if the practice be harder than the use. Where nature is mighty and therefore the victory hard, the degrees had need be, first to stay and arrest nature in time ; (like to him that would say over the four-and-twenty letters when he was angry) then to go less in quantity ;

as if one should, in forbearing wine, come from
drinking healths to a draught at a meal; and,
lastly, to discontinue altogether; but if a man
have the fortitude and resolution to enfranchise
himself at once, that is the best :—

> " Optimus ille animi vindex, lædentia pectus
>   Vincula qui rupit, dedoluitque semel."

Neither is the ancient rule amiss, to bend nature
as a wand, to a contrary extreme, whereby
to set it right; understanding it where the
contrary extreme is no vice. Let not a man
force a habit upon himself with a perpetual
continuance, but with some intermission, for
both the pause reinforceth the new onset; and
if a man that is not perfect be ever in practice,
he shall as well practise his errors as his abilities,
and induce one habit of both, and there is no
means to help this but by seasonable intermission. But let not a man trust his victory
over his nature too far, for nature will lie
buried a great time, and yet revive upon the
occasion or temptation; like as it was with
Æsop's damsel, turned from a cat to a woman,
who sat very demurely at the board's end till a
mouse ran before her; therefore, let a man
either avoid the occasion altogether or put
himself often to it, that he may be little moved
with it. A man's nature is best perceived in
privateness, for there is no affectation in passion;

for that putteth a man out of his precepts, and in a new case or experiment, for there custom leaveth him. They are happy men whose natures sort with their vocations, otherwise they may say, " Multum incola fuit anima mea " when they converse in those things they do not affect. In studies, whatsoever a man commandeth upon himself, let him set hours for it ; but whatsoever is agreeable to his nature, let him take no care for any set times ; for his thoughts will fly to it of themselves, so as the spaces of other business or studies will suffice. A man's nature runs either to herbs or weeds ; therefore let him seasonably water the one, and destroy the other.

XXXIX

OF CUSTOM AND EDUCATION

MEN'S thoughts are much according to their inclination; their discourse and speeches according to their learning and infused opinions; but their deeds are after as they have been accustomed: and, therefore, as Machiavel well noteth (though in an evil-favoured instance), there is no trusting to the force of nature, nor to the bravery of words, except it be corroborate by custom. His instance is, that for the achieving of a desperate conspiracy a man should not rest upon the fierceness of any man's nature, or his resolute undertakings, but take such a one as hath had his hands formerly in blood: but Machiavel knew not of a friar Clement, nor a Ravillac, nor a Jaureguy, nor a Baltazar Gerard; yet his rule holdeth still, that nature, nor the engagement of words, are not so forcible as custom. Only superstition is now so well advanced, that men of the first blood are as firm as butchers by occupation; and votary resolution is made equipollent to custom, even in matter of blood. In other things, the predominancy of custom is everywhere visible, insomuch as a man would wonder to hear men profess, protest, engage, give great words, and then do just as they have done before, as if they were dead images and engines, moved only by the wheels of custom. We see also the reign or tyranny of custom, what it is. The Indians (I mean the sect of their wise men) lay themselves quietly upon a stack of wood, and so sacrifice themselves by fire: nay, the wives strive to be burned with the corpse of their husbands. The lads of Sparta, of ancient time, were wont to be scourged upon the altar of Diana, without so much as queching. I remember, in the beginning of Queen Elizabeth's time of England, an Irish rebel condemned, put up a petition to the deputy that he might be hanged in a withe, and not in a halter, because it had been so used with former rebels. There be monks in Russia, for penance, that will sit a whole night in a vessel of water, till they be engaged with hard ice.

Many examples may be put of the force of custom, both upon mind and body: therefore, since custom is the principal magistrate of man's life, let men by all means endeavour to obtain good customs. Certainly, custom is most perfect when it beginneth in young years : this we call education, which is, in effect, but an early custom. So we see in languages, the tone is more pliant to all expressions and sounds, the joints are more supple to all feats of activity and motions in youth, than afterwards ; for it is true, the late learners cannot so well take up the ply, except it be in some minds, that have not suffered themselves to fix, but have kept themselves open and prepared to receive continual amendment, which is exceeding rare : but if the force of custom, simple and separate, be great, the force of custom, copulate and conjoined, and collegiate, is far greater ; for there example teacheth, company comforteth, emulation quickeneth, glory raiseth ; so as in such places the force of custom is in his exaltation. Certainly, the great multiplication of virtues upon human nature resteth upon societies well ordained and disciplined ; for commonwealths and good governments do nourish virtue grown, but do not much mend the seeds : but the misery is, that the most effectual means are now applied to the ends least to be desired.

XL

OF FORTUNE

It cannot be denied but outward accidents conduce much to fortune; favour, opportunity, death of others, occasion fitting virtue: but chiefly the mould of a man's fortune is in his own hands. "Faber quisque fortunæ suæ," saith the poet, and the most frequent of external causes is that the folly of one man is the fortune of another; for no man prospers so suddenly as by others' errors; "serpens nisi serpentem comederit non fit draco." Overt and apparent virtues bring forth praise; but there be secret and hidden virtues that bring forth fortune; certain deliveries of a man's self, which have no name. The Spanish name, "disemboltura," partly expresseth them, when there be not stonds and restiveness in a man's nature, but that the wheels of his mind keep way with the wheels of his fortune; for so Livy (after he had described Cato Major in these words, "in illo viro, tantum robur corporis et animi fuit, ut quocunque loco natus esset, fortunam sibi facturus videretur ") falleth upon that he had " versatile ingenium." Therefore, if a man look sharply and attentively, he shall see fortune ; for though she be blind, yet she is not invisible. The way of fortune is like the milken way in the sky ; which is a meeting, or knot, of a number of small stars, not seen asunder, but giving light together : so are there a number of little and scarce discerned virtues, or rather faculties and customs that make men fortunate ; the Italians note some of them, such as a man would little think. When they speak of one that cannot do amiss, they will throw in into his other conditions, that he hath " Poco di matto "; and, certainly, there be not two more fortunate properties than to have a little of the fool, and not too much of the honest : therefore extreme lovers of their country, or masters, were never fortunate ; neither can they be ; for when a man placeth his thoughts without himself, he goeth not his own way. A hasty fortune maketh an enterpriser and remover (the French hath it better, " entreprenant," or " remuant "), but the exercised fortune maketh the able man. Fortune is to be honoured and respected, and it be but for her daughters, Conscience and Reputation ; for those two felicity breedeth : the first within a man's self, the latter in others towards him. All wise men, to decline the envy of their own virtues, use to ascribe them to Providence and Fortune; for so they may the better assume them: and besides, it is greatness in a man to be the care of the higher powers. So Cæsar said to the pilot in the tempest, "Cæsarem portas, et fortunam ejus." So Sylla chose the name of "felix" and not of "magnus": and it hath been noted, that those who ascribe openly too much to their own wisdom and policy end unfortunate. It is written that Timotheus the Athenian, after he had, in the account he gave to the State of his government, often interlaced this speech, "And in this fortune had no part," never prospered in anything he undertook afterward. Certainly there be whose fortunes are like Homer's verses, that have a slide and an easiness more than the verses of other poets; as Plutarch saith of Timoleon's fortune, in respect of that of Agesilaus, or Epaminondas; and that this should be, no doubt it is much in a man's self.

XLI

OF USURY

MANY have made witty invectives against usury. They say, that it is pity the devil should have God's part, which is the tithe ; that the usurer is the greatest Sabbath-breaker, because his plough goeth every Sunday ; that the usurer is the drone that Virgil speaketh of :

" Ignavum fucos pecus a præsepibus arcent ; "

that the usurer breaketh the first law that was made for mankind after the fall, which was, " In sudore vultus tui comedes panem tuum," not " In sudore vultus alieni ; " that usurers should have orange-tawny bonnets, because they do judaize ; that it is against nature for money to beget money ; and the like. I say this only, that usury is a " concessum propter duritiem cordis : " for since there must be borrowing and lending, and men are so hard of heart as they will not lend freely, usury must be

permitted. Some others have made suspicious
and cunning propositions of banks, discovery
of men's estates, and other inventions ; but
few have spoken of usury usefully. It is good
to set before us the incommodities and commodities of usury, that the good may be either
weighed out or culled out ; and warily to
provide, that, while we make forth to that
which is better, we meet not with that which
is worse.

The discommodities of usury are, first, that
it makes fewer merchants : for were it not for
this lazy trade of usury, money would not lie
still, but it would in great part be employed
upon merchandising, which is the *vena porta*
of wealth in a State : the second, that it makes
poor merchants ; for as a farmer cannot husband his ground so well if he sit at a great
rent, so the merchant cannot drive his trade
so well if he sit at great usury : the third is
incident to the other two, and that is, the
decay of customs of kings, or estates, which
ebb or flow with merchandising : the fourth,
that it bringeth the treasure of a realm or
State into a few hands ; for the usurer being
at certainties, and the other at uncertainties,
at the end of the game most of the money
will be in the box, and ever a State flourisheth
when wealth is more equally spread : the fifth,
that it beats down the price of land ; for the

employment of money is chiefly either merchandising, or purchasing ; and usury waylays
both : the sixth, that it doth dull and damp all
industries, improvements, and new inventions,
wherein money would be stirring, if it were
not for this slug : the last, that it is the canker
and ruin of many men's estates, which in process of time breeds a public poverty.

On the other side, the commodities of usury
are, first, that howsoever usury in some respects
hindereth merchandising, yet in some other it
advanceth it, for it is certain that the greatest
part of trade is driven by young merchants
upon borrowing at interest ; so as if the usurer
either call in or keep back his money, there will
ensue presently a great stand of trade : the
second is, that, were it not for this easy borrowing upon interest, men's necessities would draw
upon them a most sudden undoing, in that
they would be forced to sell their means (be
it lands or goods) far under foot, and so,
whereas usury doth but gnaw upon them, bad
markets would swallow them quite up. As
for mortgaging, or pawning, it will little mend
the matter ; for either men will not take pawns
without use, or if they do, they will look pre-
cisely for the forfeiture. I remember a cruel
monied man in the country, that would say,
" The devil take this usury, it keeps us from
forfeitures of mortgages and bonds." The third

and last is, that it is a vanity to conceive that there would be ordinary borrowing without profit, and it is impossible to conceive the number of inconveniences that will ensue, if borrowing be cramped : therefore to speak of the abolishing of usury is idle : all States have ever had it in one kind or rate or other—so as that opinion must be sent to Utopia.

To speak now of the reformation and reglement of usury, how the discommodities of it may be best avoided, and the commodities retained. It appears by the balance of commodities and discommodities, of usury, two things are to be reconciled ; the one that the tooth of usury be grinded, that it bite not too much ; the other that there be left open a means to invite monied men to lend to the merchants, for the continuing and quickening of trade. This cannot be done, except you introduce two several sorts of usury, a less and a greater ; for if you reduce usury to one low rate, it will ease the common borrower, but the merchant will be to seek for money ; and it is to be noted, that the trade of merchandise being the most lucrative, may bear usury at a good rate—other contracts not so.

To serve both intentions, the way would be briefly thus :—that there be two rates of usury ; the one free and general for all, the other under licence only to certain persons,

and in certain places of merchandising. First,
therefore, let usury in general be reduced to
five in the hundred, and let that rate be pro-
claimed to be free and current, and let the
State shut itself out to take any penalty for
the same. This will preserve borrowing from
any general stop or dryness—this will ease
infinite borrowers in the country—this will,
in good part, raise the price of land, because
land purchased at sixteen years' purchase will
yield six in the hundred, and somewhat more,
whereas this rate of interest yields but five—
this, by like reason, will encourage and edge
industrious and profitable improvements, because many will rather venture in that kind, than
take five in the hundred, especially having been
used to greater profit. Secondly, let there
be certain persons licenced to lend to known
merchants upon usury, at a high rate, and let
it be with the cautions following. Let the
rate be, even with the merchant himself, somewhat more easy than that he used formerly to
pay ; for by that means all borrowers shall have
some ease by this reformation, be he merchant
or whosoever—let it be no bank, or common
stock, but every man be master of his own
money ; not that I altogether mislike banks,
but they will hardly be brooked, in regard of
certain suspicions. Let the State be answered
some small matter for the licence, and the

rest left to the lender; for if the abatement be but small, it will no whit discourage the lender; for he, for example, that took before ten or nine in the hundred, will sooner descend to eight in the hundred, than give over this trade of usury, and go from certain gains to gains of hazard. Let these licenced lenders be in number indefinite, but restrained to certain principal cities and towns of merchandising; for then they will be hardly able to colour other men's monies in the country, so as the licence of nine will not suck away the current rate of five; for no man will lend his monies far off, nor put them into unknown hands.

If it be objected that this doth in any sort authorize usury, which before was in some places but permissive, the answer is, that it is better to mitigate usury by declaration, than to suffer it to rage by connivance.

XLII

OF YOUTH AND AGE

A MAN that is young in years may be old in hours, if he have lost no time ; but that happeneth rarely. Generally, youth is like the first cogitations, not so wise as the second, for there is a youth in thoughts as well as in ages ; and yet the invention of young men is more lively than that of old, and imaginations stream into their minds better, and, as it were, more divinely. Natures that have much heat, and great and violent desires and perturbations, are not ripe for action till they have passed the meridian of their years ; as it was with Julius Cæsar and Septimius Severus, of the latter of whom it is said, "Juventutem egit, erroribus, imo furoribus plenam:" and yet he was the ablest emperor almost of all the list; but reposed natures may do well in youth, as it is seen in Augustus Cæsar, Cosmus Duke of Florence, Gaston de Foix, and others. On the other side, heat and vivacity in age is an excellent composition for business. Young

men are fitter to invent than to judge, fitter
for execution than for counsel, and fitter for
new projects than for settled business; for
the experience of age, in things that fall within
the compass of it, directeth them, but in new
things abuseth them. The errors of young
men are the ruin of business, but the errors
of aged men amount but to this—that more
might have been done, or sooner. Young
men, in the conduct and manage of actions,
embrace more than they can hold; stir more
than they can quiet; fly to the end, without consideration of the means and degrees;
pursue some few principles which they have
chanced upon, absurdly; care not to innovate,
which draws unknown inconveniences; use
extreme remedies at first; and that, which
doubleth all errors, will not acknowledge or
retract them, like an unready horse that will
neither stop nor turn. Men of age object
too much, consult too long, adventure too
little, repent too soon, and seldom drive business home to the full period, but content
themselves with a mediocrity of success. Certainly it is good to compound employments
of both; for that will be good for the present,
because the virtues of either age may correct
the defects of both; and good for succession,
that young men may be learners, while men
in age are actors; and, lastly, good for extern

accidents, because authority followeth old men,
and favour and popularity youth ; but, for the
moral part, perhaps, youth will have the pre-
eminence, as age hath for the politic. A
certain rabbin, upon the text, " Your young
men shall see visions, and your old men shall
dream dreams," inferreth that young men are
admitted nearer to God than old, because
vision is a clearer revelation than a dream ;
and, certainly, the more a man drinketh of
the world, the more it intoxicateth ; and age
doth profit rather in the powers of understanding, than in the virtues of the will and
affections. There be some have an over-early
ripeness in their years, which fadeth betimes :
these are first, such as have brittle wits,
the edge whereof is soon turned ; such as
was Hermogenes the rhetorician, whose books
are exceedingly subtle, who afterwards waxed
stupid : a second sort is of those that have
some natural dispositions, which have better
grace in youth than in age, such as is a fluent
and luxurious speech, which becomes youth
well, but not age ; so Tully saith of Hortensius,
" Idem manebat, neque idem decebat : " the
third is of such as take too high a strain at the
first, and are magnanimous more than tract of
years can uphold ; as was Scipio Africanus,
of whom Livy saith in effect, " Ultima primis
cedebant."

XLIII

OF BEAUTY

VIRTUE is like a rich stone, best plain set ; and surely virtue is best in a body that is comely, though not of delicate features, and that hath rather dignity of presence than beauty of aspect ; neither is it almost seen that very beautiful persons are otherwise of great virtue, as if nature were rather busy not to err, than in labour to produce excellency, and therefore they prove accomplished, but not of great spirit, and study rather behaviour than virtue. But this holds not always ; for Augustus Cæsar, Titus Vespasianus, Philip le Bel of France, Edward IV. of England, Alcibiades of Athens, Ismael the sophy of Persia, were all high and great spirits, and yet the most beautiful men of their times. In beauty, that of favour is more than that of colour, and that of decent and gracious motion more than that of favour. That is the best part of beauty which a picture cannot express, no, nor the first sight of the life. There is no excellent beauty that hath not some strangeness in the proportion. A man cannot tell whether Apelles or Albert Dürer were the more trifler ; whereof the one would make a personage by geometrical proportions, the other, by taking the best parts out of divers faces, to make one excellent. Such personages, I think, would please nobody but the painter that made them—not but I think a painter may make a better face than ever was, but he must do it by a kind of felicity (as a musician that maketh an excellent air in music), and not by rule. A man shall see faces, that if you examine them part by part you shall find never a good, and yet altogether do well. If it be true that the principal part of beauty is in decent motion, certainly it is no marvel though persons in years seem many times more amiable : " Pulchrorum autumnus pulcher "—for no youth can be comely but by pardon, and considering the youth as to make up the comeliness. Beauty is as summer-fruits, which are easy to corrupt, and cannot last, and, for the most part, it makes a dissolute youth, and an age a little out of countenance ; but yet certainly again, if it light well, it maketh virtue shine, and vices blush.

XLIV

OF DEFORMITY

DEFORMED persons are commonly even with nature ; for as nature hath done ill by them, so do they by nature, being for the most part (as the Scripture saith) " void of natural affection " : and so they have their revenge of nature. Certainly there is a consent between the body and the mind, and " where nature erreth in the one she ventureth in the other " (" Ubi peccat in uno, periclitatur in altero ") : but because there is in man an election touching the frame of his mind, and a necessity in the frame of his body, the stars of natural inclination are sometimes obscured by the sun of discipline and virtue ; therefore, it is good to consider of deformity, not as a sign which is more deceivable, but as a cause which seldom faileth of the effect. Whosoever hath anything fixed in his person that doth induce contempt, hath also a perpetual spur in himself to rescue and deliver himself from scorn ; therefore, all deformed persons are extreme bold—first, as in their own defence, as being exposed to scorn, but in process of time by a general habit. Also, it stirreth in them industry, and especially of this kind, to watch and observe the weakness of others, that they may have somewhat to repay. Again, in their superiors, it quencheth jealousy towards them, as persons that they think they may at pleasure despise; and it layeth their competitors and emulators asleep, as never believing they should be in possibility of advancement, till they see them in possession; so that upon the matter, in a great wit, deformity is an advantage to rising. Kings, in ancient times (and at this present, in some countries), were wont to put great trust in eunuchs, because they that are envious towards all are obnoxious and officious towards one: but yet their trust towards them hath rather been as to good spials and good whisperers than good magistrates and officers; and much like is the reason of deformed persons. Still the ground is, they will, if they be of spirit, seek to free themselves from scorn, which must be either by virtue or malice; and therefore, let it not be marvelled, if sometimes they prove excellent persons; as was Agesilaus, Zanger the son of Solyman, Æsop, Gasca, president of Peru; and Socrates may go likewise amongst them, with others.

XLV

OF BUILDING

HOUSES are built to live in, and not to look on; therefore, let use be preferred before uniformity, except where both may be had. Leave the goodly fabrics of houses, for beauty, only to the enchanted palaces of the poets, who build them with small cost. He that builds a fair house upon an ill seat committeth himself to prison—neither do I reckon it an ill seat only where the air is unwholesome, but likewise where the air is unequal; as you shall see many fine seats set upon a knap of ground, environed with higher hills round about it, whereby the heat of the sun is pent in, and the wind gathereth as in troughs; so as you shall have, and that suddenly, as great diversity of heat and cold as if you dwelt in several places. Neither is it ill air only that maketh an ill seat, but ill ways, ill markets; and if you consult with Momus, ill neighbours. I speak not of many more; want of water

want of wood, shade, and shelter, want of
fruitfulness, and mixture of grounds of several
natures; want of prospect, want of level
grounds, want of places at some near distance
for sports of hunting, hawking, and races; too
near the sea, too remote; having the commodity of navigable rivers, or the discommodity
of their overflowing; too far off from great
cities, which may hinder business; or too near
them, which lurcheth all provisions, and maketh
everything dear; where a man hath a great
living laid together, and where he is scanted;
all which, as it is impossible perhaps to find
together, so it is good to know them, and
think of them, that a man may take as many as
he can; and, if he have several dwellings, that
he sort them so, that what he wanteth in the
one he may find in the other. Lucullus
answered Pompey well, who, when he saw his
stately galleries and rooms so large and lightsome, in one of his houses, said, " Surely, an
excellent place for summer, but how do you in
winter ? " Lucullus answered, " Why do you
not think me as wise as some fowls are, that
ever change their abode towards the winter ? "

To pass from the seat to the house itself, we
will do as Cicero doth in the orator's art, who
writes books *De Oratore*, and a book he entitles
Orator; whereof the former delivers the precepts of the art, and the latter the perfection.

We will therefore describe a princely palace, making a brief model thereof; for it is strange to see, now in Europe, such huge buildings as the Vatican and Escurial, and some others be, and yet scarce a very fair room in them.

First, therefore, I say, you cannot have a perfect palace, except you have two several sides; a side for the banquet, as is spoken of in the book of Esther, and a side for the household; the one for feasts and triumphs, and the other for dwelling. I understand both these sides to be not only returns, but parts of the front; and to be uniform without, though severally partitioned within; and to be on both sides of a great and stately tower in the midst of the front, that, as it were, joineth them together on either hand. I would have, on the side of the banquet in front, one only goodly room above stairs, of some forty feet high; and under it a room for a dressing, or preparing place, at times of triumphs. On the other side, which is the household side, I wish it divided at the first into a hall and a chapel, with a partition between, both of good state and bigness, and those not to go all the length, but to have at the farther end a winter and a summer parlour, both fair; and under these rooms a fair and large cellar sunk under ground; and likewise some privy kitchens, with butteries and pantries, and the like. As for the tower,

I would have it two stories, of eighteen feet high apiece above the two wings; and goodly leads upon the top, railed with statues interposed; and the same tower to be divided into rooms, as shall be thought fit. The stairs likewise to the upper rooms, let them be upon a fair and open newel, and finely railed in with images of wood cast into a brass colour, and a very fair landing place at the top. But this to be, if you do not point any of the lower rooms for a dining place of servants; for otherwise, you shall have the servants' dinner after your own, for the steam of it will come up as in a tunnel. And so much for the front, only I understand the height of the first stairs to be sixteen feet, which is the height of the lower room.

Beyond this front is there to be a fair court, but three sides of it of a far lower building than the front; and in all the four corners of that court fair staircases, cast into turrets on the outside, and not within the rows of buildings themselves; but those towers are not to be of the height of the front, but rather proportionable to the lower building. Let the court not be paved, for that striketh up a great heat in summer, and much cold in winter, but only some side alleys with a cross, and the quarters to graze, being kept shorn, but not too near shorn. The row of return on the banquet side, let it be all stately galleries ; in which galleries let there be three or five fine cupolas in the length of it, placed at equal distance, and fine coloured windows of several works ; on the household side, chambers of presence and ordinary entertainments, with some bedchambers ; and let all three sides be a double house, without thorough lights on the sides, that you may have rooms from the sun, both for forenoon and afternoon. Cast it also that you may have rooms both for summer and winter, shady for summer and warm for winter. You shall have sometimes fair houses so full of glass, that one cannot tell where to be become to be out of the sun or cold. For embowed windows, I hold them of good use ; in cities, indeed, upright do better, in respect of the uniformity towards the street ; for they be pretty retiring places for conference, and, besides, they keep both the wind and sun off— for that which would strike almost through the room doth scarce pass the window ; but let them be but few, four in the court, on the sides only.

Beyond this court, let there be an inward court, of the same square and height, which is to be environed, with the garden on all sides ; and in the inside, cloistered on all sides upon decent and beautiful arches, as high as the first storey ; on the under storey, towards the

garden, let it be turned to a grotto, or place of
shade, or estivation ; and only have opening
and windows towards the garden, and be level
upon the floor, no whit sunk under ground, to
avoid all dampishness ; and let there be a
fountain, or some fair work of statues in the
midst of the court, and to be paved as the
other court was. These buildings to be for
privy lodgings on both sides, and the end for
privy galleries ; whereof you must foresee that
one of them be for an infirmary, if the prince
or any special person should be sick, with
chambers, bed-chamber, " antecamera " [" anti-
chamber "], and " recamera," [" retiring-
chamber," or " back-chamber "] joining to it ;
this upon the second storey. Upon the ground
storey, a fair gallery, open, upon pillars ; and
upon the third storey likewise, an open gallery
upon pillars, to take the prospect and freshness
of the garden. At both corners of the farther
side, by way of return, let there be two delicate
or rich cabinets, daintily paved, richly hanged,
glazed with crystalline glass, and a rich cupola
in the midst, and all other elegancy that may
be thought upon. In the upper gallery, too, I
wish that there may be, if the place will yield
it, some fountains running in divers places from
the wall, with some fine avoidances. And thus
much for the model of the palace ; save that you
must have, before you come to the front, three

courts—a green court plain, with a wall about it ; a second court of the same, but more garnished with little turrets, or rather embellishments, upon the wall ; and a third court, to make a square with the front, but not to be built, nor yet enclosed with a naked wall, but enclosed with terraces leaded aloft, and fairly garnished on the three sides, and cloistered on the inside with pillars, and not with arches below. As for offices, let them stand at distance, with some low galleries to pass from them to the palace itself.

XLVI

OF GARDENS

GOD ALMIGHTY first planted a garden, and, indeed, it is the purest of human pleasures; it is the greatest refreshment to the spirits of man, without which buildings and palaces are but gross handyworks: and a man shall ever see, that when ages grow to civility and elegancy, men come to build stately, sooner than to garden finely; as if gardening were the greater perfection. I do hold it, in the royal ordering of gardens, there ought to be gardens for all the months in the year, in which, severally, things of beauty may be then in season. For December and January, and the latter part of November, you must take such things as are green all winter; holly, ivy, bays, juniper, cypress-trees, yew, pines, fir-trees, rosemary, lavender; periwinkle, the white, the purple, and the blue; germander, flag, orange-trees, lemon-trees, and myrtles, if they be stoved; and sweet marjoram, warm set. There

followeth, for the latter part of January and
February, the mezereon tree, which then blos-
soms; crocus vernus, both the yellow and
the grey; primroses, anemones, the early tulip,
hyacinthus orientalis, chamaïris, fritellaria. For
March, there come violets, especially the single
blue, which are the earliest; the early daffodil, the daisy, the almond-tree in blossom,
the peach-tree in blossom, the cornelian-tree
in blossom, sweetbriar. In April, follow the
double white violet, the wallflower, the stock-
gilliflower, the cowslip, flower-de-luces, and
lilies of all natures; rosemary-flowers, the tulip,
the double peony, the pale daffodil, the French
honeysuckle, the cherry-tree in blossom, the
damascene and plum-trees in blossom, the
white thorn in leaf, the lilac-tree. In May
and June come pinks of all sorts, especially the
blush pink; roses of all kinds, except the musk,
which comes later; honeysuckles, strawberries,
bugloss, columbine, the French marigold, flos
Africanus, cherry-tree in fruit, ribes, figs in
fruit, rasps, vine flowers, lavender in flowers,
the sweet satyrian, with the white flower:
herba muscaria, lilium convallium, and apple-
tree in blossom. In July come gilliflowers of all
varieties, musk roses, the lime-tree in blossom,
early pears, and plums in fruit, gennitings,
quodlins. In August come plums of all sorts
in fruit, pears, apricocks, barberries, filberds,

musk melons, monks-hoods, of all colours. In
September come grapes, apples, poppies of all
colours, peaches, melocotones, nectarines, cor-
nelians, wardens, quinces.   In October and the
beginning of November come services, medlars,
bullaces, roses cut or removed to come late,
hollyoaks, and suchlike. These particulars are
for the climate of London ; but my meaning is
perceived, that you may have *ver perpetuum*, as
the place affords.

And because the breath of flowers is far
sweeter in the air (where it comes and goes,
like the warbling of music) than in the hand,
therefore nothing is more fit for that delight,
than to know what be the flowers and plants
that do best perfume the air. Roses, damask
and red, are fast flowers of their smells ; so that
you may walk by a whole row of them, and
find nothing of their sweetness, yea, though it
be in a morning's dew. Bays, likewise, yield
no smell as they grow, rosemary little, nor
sweet marjoram ; that which, above all others,
yields the sweetest smell in the air is the violet ;
especially the white double violet, which comes
twice a-year—about the middle of April, and
about Bartholomew-tide. Next to that is the
musk rose ; then the strawberry leaves dying,
with a most excellent cordial smell ; then the
flower of the vines—it is a little dust like the
dust of a bent, which grows upon the cluster

in the first coming forth—then sweetbriar,
then wallflowers, which are very delightful
to be set under a parlour or lower chamber
window ; then pinks and gilliflowers, especially
the matted pink and clove gilliflowers ; then
the flowers of the lime-tree ; then the honeysuckles, so they be somewhat afar off. Of
bean-flowers I speak not, because they are field
flowers ; but those which perfume the air most
delightfully, not passed by as the rest, but
being trodden upon and crushed, are three,
that is, burnet, wild thyme, and water-mints ;
therefore, you are to set whole alleys of them,
to have the pleasure when you walk or tread.

For gardens (speaking of those which are,
indeed, prince-like, as we have done of buildings), the contents ought not well to be under
thirty acres of ground, and to be divided into
three parts ; a green in the entrance, a heath
or desert in the going forth, and the main
garden in the midst, besides alleys on both
sides ; and I like well that four acres of ground
be assigned to the green, six to the heath, four
and four to either side, and twelve to the main
garden. The green hath two pleasures : the
one, because nothing is more pleasant to the
eye than green grass kept finely shorn ; the
other, because it will give you a fair alley in
the midst, by which you may go in front upon
a stately hedge, which is to enclose the garden :

but because the alley will be long, and, in great
heat of the year, or day, you ought not to buy
the shade in the garden by going in the sun
through the green, therefore you are, of either
side the green, to plant a covert alley, upon
carpenters' work, about twelve feet in height,
by which you may go in shade into the garden.
As for the making of knots, or figures, with
divers-coloured earths, that they may lie under
the windows of the house on that side on
which the garden stands, they be but toys:
you may see as good sights many times in tarts.
The garden is best to be square, encompassed
on all the four sides with a stately arched
hedge; the arches to be upon pillars of carpenters' work, of some ten feet high, and six
feet broad, and the spaces between of the
same dimensions with the breadth of the arch.
Over the arches let there be an entire hedge
of some four feet high, framed also upon
carpenters' work; and upon the upper hedge,
over every arch, a little turret, with a belly
enough to receive a cage of birds: and over
every space between the arches some other
little figure, with broad plates of round coloured
glass gilt, for the sun to play upon: but this
hedge I intend to be raised upon a bank, not
steep, but gently slope, of some six feet, set
all with flowers. Also, I understand that this
square of the garden should not be the whole

breadth of the ground, but to leave on either side ground enough for diversity of side alleys, unto which the two covert alleys of the green may deliver you ; but there must be no alleys with hedges at either end of this great enclosure —not at the hither end, for letting your prospect upon this fair hedge from the green—nor at the farther end, for letting your prospect from the hedge through the arches upon the heath.

For the ordering of the ground within the great hedge, I leave it to variety of device, advising, nevertheless, that whatsoever form you cast it into first, it be not too busy, or full of work ; wherein I, for my part, do not like images cut out in juniper or other garden stuff—they be for children. Little low hedges, round like welts, with some pretty pyramids, I like well ; and in some places fair columns, upon frames of carpenters' work. I would also have the alleys spacious and fair. You may have closer alleys upon the side grounds, but none in the main garden. I wish, also, in the very middle, a fair mount, with three ascents and alleys, enough for four to walk abreast, which I would have to be perfect circles, without any bulwarks or embossments ; and the whole mount to be thirty feet high, and some fine banqueting-house, with some chimneys neatly cast, and without too much glass.

For fountains they are a great beauty and refreshment; but pools mar all, and make the garden unwholesome, and full of flies and frogs. Fountains I intend to be of two natures, the one that sprinkleth or spouteth water; the other a fair receipt of water, of some thirty or forty feet square, but without any fish, or slime, or mud. For the first, the ornaments of images, gilt, or of marble, which are in use, do well; but the main matter is so to convey the water as it never stay, either in the bowls or in the cistern—that the water be never by rest discoloured, green or red, or the like, or gather any mossiness or putrefaction; besides that, it is to be cleansed every day by the hand—also some steps up to it, and some fine pavement about it do well. As for the other kind of fountain, which we may call a bathing pool, it may admit much curiosity and beauty, where-with we will not trouble ourselves: as, that the bottom be finely paved, and with images; the sides likewise; and withal embellished with coloured glass, and such things of lustre, en-compassed also with fine rails of low statuas; but the main point is the same which we men-tioned in the former kind of fountain, which is, that the water be in perpetual motion, fed by a water higher than the pool, and delivered into it by fair spouts, and then discharged away under ground, by some equality of bores, that it stay little; and for fine devices of arching water without spilling, and making it rise in several forms (of feathers, drinking glasses, canopies, and the like), they be pretty things to look on, but nothing to health and sweetness.

For the heath, which was the third part of our plot, I wished it to be framed as much as may be to a natural wildness. Trees I would have none in it, but some thickets made only of sweetbriar and honeysuckle, and some wild vines amongst, and the ground set with violets, strawberries, and primroses; for these are sweet, and prosper in the shade, and these are to be in the heath here and there, not in any order. I like also little heaps, in the nature of mole-hills (such as are in wild heaths), to be set, some with wild thyme, some with pinks, some with germander, that gives a good flower to the eye; some with periwinkle, some with violets, some with strawberries, some with cowslips, some with daisies, some with red roses, some with lilium convallium, some with sweet-williams red, some with bear's-foot, and the like low flowers, being withal sweet and sightly —part of which heaps to be with standards of little bushes pricked upon their top, and part without—the standards to be roses, juniper, holly, berberries (but here and there, because of the smell of their blossom), red currents, gooseberries, rosemary, bays, sweetbriar, and suchlike; but these standards to be kept with cutting, that they grow not out of course.

For the side grounds, you are to fill them with variety of alleys, private to give a full shade; some of them wheresoever the sun be. You are to frame some of them likewise for shelter, that, when the wind blows sharp, you may walk as in a gallery; and those alleys must be likewise hedged at both ends, to keep out the wind, and these closer alleys must be ever finely gravelled, and no grass, because of going wet. In many of these alleys, likewise, you are to set fruit-trees of all sorts, as well upon the walls as in ranges; and this should be generally observed, that the borders wherein you plant your fruit-trees be fair, and large, and low, and not steep, and set with fine flowers, but thin and sparingly, lest they deceive the trees. At the end of both the side grounds I would have a mount of some pretty height, leaving the wall of the enclosure breast-high, to look abroad into the fields.

For the main garden, I do not deny but there should be some fair alleys ranged on both sides, with fruit-trees, and some pretty tufts of fruit-trees and arbours with seats, set in some decent order; but these to be by no means set too thick, but to leave the main garden so as it be not close, but the air open

and free. For as for shade, I would have you
rest upon the alleys of the side grounds, there
to walk, if you be disposed, in the heat of the
year or day ; but to make account, that the
main garden is for the more temperate parts of
the year, and, in the heat of summer, for the
morning and the evening, or overcast days.

For aviaries, I like them not, except they be
of that largeness as they may be turfed, and
have living plants and bushes set in them,
that the birds may have more scope and
natural nestling, and that no foulness appear
on the floor of the aviary. So I have made
a platform of a princely garden, partly by
precept, partly by drawing—not a model, but
some general lines of it—and in this I have
spared for no cost ; but it is nothing for great
princes, that, for the most part, taking advice
with workmen, with no less cost, set their
things together, and sometimes add statues,
and such things, for state and magnificence,
but nothing to the true pleasure of a garden.

XLVII

OF NEGOTIATING

IT is generally better to deal by speech than by letter, and by the mediation of a third than by a man's self. Letters are good, when a man would draw an answer by letter back again, or when it may serve for a man's justification afterward to produce his own letter: or where it may be danger to be interrupted, or heard by pieces. To deal in person is good, when a man's face breedeth regard, as commonly with inferiors ; or in tender cases, where a man's eye upon the countenance of him with whom he speaketh may give him a direction how far to go ; and generally, where a man will reserve to himself liberty, either to disavow or expound. In choice of instruments, it is better to chuse men of a plainer sort, that are like to do that that is committed to them, and to report back again faithfully the success, than those that are cunning to contrive out of other men's business somewhat to grace themselves, and will help the matter in report, for satisfaction sake. Use also such persons as affect the business wherein they are employed, for that quickeneth much ; and such as are fit for the matter, as bold men for expostulation, fair-spoken men for persuasion, crafty men for inquiry and observation, froward and absurd men for business that doth not well bear out itself. Use also such as have been lucky, and prevailed before in things wherein you have employed them ; for that breeds confidence, and they will strive to maintain their prescription.

It is better to sound a person with whom one deals, afar off, than to fall upon the point at first, except you mean to surprise him by some short question. It is better dealing with men in appetite, than with those that are where they would be. If a man deals with another upon conditions, the start of first performance is all ; which a man cannot reasonably demand, except either the nature of the thing be such which must go before ; or else a man can persuade the other party, that he shall still need him in some other thing ; or else that he be counted the honester man. All practice is to discover, or to work. Men discover themselves in trust, in passion, at unawares ; and of necessity, when they would have somewhat done, and cannot find an apt pretext. If you would work any man, you must either know his nature or fashions, and so lead him ; or his ends, and so persuade him ; or his weakness and disadvantages, and so awe him ; or those that have interest in him, and so govern him. In dealing with cunning persons, we must ever consider their ends to interpret their speeches ; and it is good to say little to them, and that which they least look for. In all negotiations of difficulty, a man may not look to sow and reap at once, but must prepare business, and so ripen it by degrees.

XLVIII

OF FOLLOWERS AND FRIENDS

COSTLY followers are not to be liked, lest, while a man maketh his train longer, he makes his wings shorter. I reckon to be costly, not them alone which charge the purse, but which are wearisome and importune in suits. Ordinary followers ought to challenge no higher conditions than countenance, recommendation, and protection from wrongs. Factious followers are worse to be liked, which follow not upon affection to him with whom they range themselves, but upon discontentment conceived against some other; whereupon commonly ensueth that ill intelligence that we many times see between great personages. Likewise glorious followers, who make themselves as trumpets of the commendation of those they follow, are full of inconvenience, for they taint business through want of secrecy; and they export honour from a man, and make him a return in envy. There is a kind of followers,

likewise, which are dangerous, being indeed
espials, which inquire the secrets of the house,
and bear tales of them to others ; yet such men
many times are in great favour, for they are
officious, and commonly exchange tales. The
following by certain estates of men, answerable
to that which a great man himself professeth
(as of soldiers to him that hath been employed
in the wars, and the like), hath ever been a
thing civil, and well taken even in monarchies,
so it be without too much pomp or popularity :
but the most honourable kind of following is
to be followed as one that apprehendeth to ad-
vance virtue and desert in all sorts of persons,
and yet, where there is no eminent odds in
sufficiency, it is better to take with the more
passable than with the more able : and, besides,
to speak truth in base times, active men are
of more use than virtuous. It is true, that
in government it is good to use men of one
rank equally : for to countenance some ex-
traordinarily is to make them insolent, and the
rest discontent, because they may claim a due ;
but contrariwise in favour, to use men with
much difference and election, is good ; for it
maketh the persons preferred more thankful,
and the rest more officious ; because all is of
favour. It is good discretion not to make
too much of any man at the first, because
one cannot hold out that proportion. To be

governed (as we call it), by one, is not safe, for it shows softness, and gives a freedom to scandal and disreputation ; for those that would not censure or speak ill of a man immediately, will talk more boldly of those that are so great with them, and thereby wound their honour ; yet to be distracted with many is worse, for it makes men to be of the last impression, and full of change. To take advice of some few friends is ever honourable ; for lookers-on many times see more than gamesters ; and the vale best discovereth the hill. There is little friendship in the world, and least of all between equals, which was wont to be magnified. That that is, is between superior and inferior, whose fortunes may comprehend the one the other.

XLIX

OF SUITORS

Many ill matters and projects are undertaken, and private suits do putrefy the public good. Many good matters are undertaken with bad minds—I mean not only corrupt minds, but crafty minds, that intend not performance. Some embrace suits, which never mean to deal effectually in them ; but if they see there may be life in the matter, by some other mean, they will be content to win a thank, or take a second reward, or, at least, to make use in the meantime of the suitor's hopes. Some take hold of suits only for an occasion to cross some other, or to make an information, whereof they could not otherwise have apt pretext, without care what become of the suit when the turn is served ; or, generally, to make other men's business a kind of entertainment to bring in their own ; nay, some undertake suits with a full purpose to let them fall, to the end to gratify the adverse party, or competitor.

Surely there is in some sort a right in every suit: either a right of equity, if it be a suit of controversy, or a right of desert, if it be a suit of petition. If affection lead a man to favour the wrong side in justice, let him rather use his countenance to compound the matter than to carry it. If affection lead a man to favour the less worthy in desert, let him do it without depraving or disabling the better deserver. In suits which a man doth not well understand, it is good to refer them to some friend of trust and judgment, that may report whether he may deal in them with honour; but let him chuse well his referendaries, for else he may be led by the nose. Suitors are so distasted with delays and abuses, that plain dealing in denying to deal in suits at first, and reporting the success barely, and in challenging no more thanks than one hath deserved, is grown not only honourable, but also gracious. In suits of favour, the first coming ought to take little place; so far forth consideration may be had of his trust, that if intelligence of the matter could not otherwise have been had but by him, advantage be not taken of the note, but the party left to his other means, and in some sort recompensed for his discovery. To be ignorant of the value of a suit is simplicity, as well as to be ignorant of the right thereof is want of conscience. Secrecy in suits is a great mean of

obtaining ; for voicing them to be in forwardness may discourage some kind of suitors, but
doth quicken and awake others ; but timing of
the suit is the principal—timing, I say, not only
in respect of the person who should grant it,
but in respect of those which are like to cross
it. Let a man, in the choice of his mean,
rather chuse the fittest mean than the greatest
mean ; and rather them that deal in certain
things, than those that are general. The
reparation of a denial is sometimes equal to
the first grant, if a man show himself neither
dejected nor discontented. " Iniquum petas,
ut æquum feras " is a good rule where a man
hath strength of favour ; but otherwise, a man
were better rise in his suit, for he that would
have ventured at first to have lost the suitor,
will not, in the conclusion, lose both the
suitor and his own former favour. Nothing is
thought so easy a request to a great person,
as his letter ; and yet, if it be not in a good
cause, it is so much out of his reputation.
There are no worse instruments than these
general contrivers of suits, for they are but a
kind of poison and infection to public proceedings.

L

OF STUDIES

STUDIES serve for delight, for ornament, and for ability. Their chief use for delight is in their privateness and retiring ; for ornament, is in discourse ; and for ability, is in the judgment and disposition of business ; for expert men can execute, and perhaps judge of particulars, one by one ; but the general counsels, and the plots and marshalling of affairs, come best from those that are learned. To spend too much time in studies is sloth ; to use them too much for ornament is affectation ; to make judgment wholly by their rules is the humour of a scholar ; they perfect nature, and are perfected by experience—for natural abilities are like natural plants, that need pruning by study ; and studies themselves do give forth directions too much at large, except they be bounded in by experience. Crafty men contemn studies, simple men admire them, and wise men use them, for they teach not their own use ; but that is a wisdom without them, and above them, won by observation. Read not to contradict and confute, nor to believe and take for granted, nor to find talk and discourse, but to weigh and consider. Some books are to be tasted, others to be swallowed, and some few to be chewed and digested; that is, some books are to be read only in parts; others to be read, but not curiously; and some few to be read wholly, and with diligence and attention. Some books also may be read by deputy, and extracts made of them by others; but that would be only in the less important arguments, and the meaner sort of books; else distilled books are, like common distilled waters, flashy things. Reading maketh a full man, conference a ready man, and writing an exact man; and, therefore, if a man write little, he had need have a great memory; if he confer little, he had need have a present wit; and if he read little, he had need have much cunning, to seem to know that he doth not. Histories make men wise; poets witty; the mathematics subtle; natural philosophy deep; moral, grave; logic and rhetoric, able to contend; " Abeunt studia in mores "—nay, there is no stond or impediment in the wit, but may be wrought out by fit studies, like as diseases of the body may have appropriate exercises—bowling is good for the stone and reins, shooting for the lungs and breast, gentle walking for the stomach, riding for the head, and the like; so, if a man's wits be wandering, let him study the mathematics, for in demonstrations, if his wit be called away never so little, he must begin again; if his wits be not apt to distinguish or find differences, let him study the school-men, for they are " cymini sectores "; if he be not apt to beat over matters, and to call upon one thing to prove and illustrate another, let him study the lawyers' cases—so every defect of the mind may have a special receipt.

LI

OF FACTION

MANY have an opinion not wise, that for a prince to govern his estate, or for a great person to govern his proceedings, according to the respect of factions, is a principal part of policy, whereas, contrariwise, the chiefest wisdom is, either in ordering those things which are general, and wherein men of several factions do nevertheless agree, or in dealing with correspondence to particular persons one by one. But I say not that the consideration of factions is to be neglected. Mean men, in their rising, must adhere ; but great men, that have strength in themselves, were better to maintain themselves indifferent and neutral : yet even in beginners, to adhere so moderately, as he be a man of the one faction, which is most passable with the other, commonly giveth best way. The lower and weaker faction is the firmer in conjunction ; and it is often seen that a few that are stiff do tire out a greater number that are more moderate. When one of the factions is extinguished, the remaining subdivideth; as the faction between Lucullus and the rest of the nobles of the Senate (which they called optimates) held out awhile against the faction of Pompey and Cæsar; but when the Senate's authority was pulled down, Cæsar and Pompey soon after brake. The faction, or party, of Antonius and Octavius Cæsar against Brutus and Cassius, held out likewise for a time; but when Brutus and Cassius were overthrown, then soon after Antonius and Octavius brake and subdivided. These examples are of wars, but the same holdeth in private factions; and, therefore, those that are seconds in factions do many times, when the faction subdivideth, prove principals; but many times also they prove cyphers and cashiered; for many a man's strength is in opposition, and, when that faileth, he groweth out of use. It is commonly seen that men once placed take in with the contrary faction to that by which they enter: thinking, belike, that they have their first sure, and now are ready for a new purchase. The traitor in faction lightly goeth away with it, for when matters have stuck long in balancing, the winning of some one man casteth them, and he getteth all the thanks. The even carriage between two factions proceedeth not always of moderation, but of a trueness to a man's self, with end to make use of both. Certainly, in Italy, they hold it a little suspect in popes, when they have often in their mouth, " Padre commune "; and take it to be a sign of one that meaneth to refer all to the greatness of his own house. Kings had need beware how they side themselves, and make themselves as of a faction or party; for leagues within the State are ever pernicious to monarchies; for they raise an obligation paramount to obligation of sovereignty, and make the king " tanquam unus ex nobis "; as was to be seen in the league of France. When factions are carried too high and too violently, it is a sign of weakness in princes, and much to the prejudice both of their authority and business. The motions of factions under kings ought to be like the motions (as the astronomers speak) of the inferior orbs, which may have their proper motions, but yet still are quietly carried by the higher motion of " primum mobile."

LII

OF CEREMONIES AND RESPECTS

HE that is only real had need have exceeding great parts of virtue, as the stone had need to be rich that is set without foil ; but if a man mark it well, it is in praise and commendation of men as it is in gettings and gains ; for the proverb is true, " That light gains make heavy purses," for light gains come thick, whereas great come but now and then ; so it is true, that small matters win great commendation, because they are continually in use and in note, whereas the occasion of any great virtue cometh but on festivals. Therefore it doth much add to a man's reputation, and is (as Queen Isabella said) like perpetual letters commendatory, to have good forms. To attain them, it almost sufficeth not to despise them ; for so shall a man observe them in others, and let him trust himself with the rest ; for if he labour too much to express them, he shall lose their grace, which is to be natural and unaffected. Some men's behaviour is like a verse, wherein every syllable is measured. How can a man comprehend great matters, that breaketh his mind too much to small observations? Not to use ceremonies at all is to teach others not to use them again, and so diminish respect to himself; especially they are not to be omitted to strangers and formal natures; but the dwelling upon them, and exalting them above the moon, is not only tedious, but both diminish the faith and credit of him that speaks; and, certainly, there is a kind of conveying of effectual and imprinting passages amongst compliments, which is of singular use, if a man can hit upon it. Amongst a man's peers a man shall be sure of familiarity, and therefore it is good a little to keep state; amongst a man's inferiors one shall be sure of reverence, and therefore it is good a little to be familiar. He that is too much in any thing, so that he giveth another occasion of satiety, maketh himself cheap. To apply one's self to others is good, so it be with demonstration, that a man doth it upon regard and not upon facility. It is a good precept generally in seconding another, yet to add somewhat of one's own; as if you will grant his opinion, let it be with some distinction; if you will follow his motion, let it be with condition; if you allow his counsel, let it be with alleging further reason. Men had need beware how they be too perfect in compliments, for be they never so sufficient otherwise, their enviers will be sure to give them that attribute, to the disadvantage of their greater virtues. It is loss also in business to be too full of respects, or to be too curious in observing times and opportunities. Solomon saith, " He that considereth the wind shall not sow, and he that looketh to the clouds shall not reap." A wise man will make more opportunities than he finds. Men's behaviour should be like their apparel, not too strait or point device, but free for exercise or motion.

LIII

OF PRAISE

PRAISE is the reflection of virtue, but it is as the glass, or body, which giveth the reflection; if it be from the common people, it is commonly false and naught, and rather followeth vain persons than virtuous; for the common people understand not many excellent virtues: the lowest virtues draw praise from them, the middle virtues work in them astonishment or admiration; but of the highest virtues they have no sense or perceiving at all; but shows and " species virtutibus similes " serve best with them. Certainly, fame is like a river, that beareth up things light and swollen, and drowns things weighty and solid; but if persons of quality and judgment concur, then it is (as the Scripture saith), " Nomen bonum instar unguenti fragrantis; " it filleth all round about, and will not easily away; for the odours of ointments are more durable than those of flowers.

There be so many false points of praise, that a man may justly hold it in suspect. Some praises proceed merely of flattery; and if it be an ordinary flatterer, he will have certain common attributes, which may serve every man; if he be a cunning flatterer, he will follow the arch-flatterer, which is a man's self, and wherein a man thinketh best of himself, therein the flatterer will uphold him most: but if he be an impudent flatterer, look wherein a man is conscious to himself that he is most defective, and is most out of countenance in himself, that will the flatterer entitle him to, perforce, "Spreta conscientia." Some praises come of good wishes and respects, which is a form due in civility to kings and great persons, "laudando præcipere"; when by telling them what they are, they represent to them what they should be. Some men are praised maliciously to their hurt, thereby to stir envy and jealousy towards them; "pessimum genus inimicorum laudantium;" inasmuch as it was a proverb amongst the Grecians that "He that was praised to his hurt should have a push rise upon his nose;" as we say, that a blister will rise upon one's tongue that tells a lie. Certainly moderate praise, used with opportunity, and not vulgar, is that which doeth the good. Solomon saith, he that praiseth his friend aloud, rising early, it shall be to him no better than a curse. Too much magnifying of man or matter doth irritate contradiction, and procure envy and scorn. To praise a man's self cannot be decent, except it be in rare cases; but to praise a man's office or profession, he may do it with good grace, and with a kind of magnanimity. The cardinals of Rome, which are theologues, and friars, and schoolmen, have a phrase of notable contempt and scorn towards civil business; for they call all temporal business of wars, embassages, judicature, and other employments, sherrerie, which is under sheriffries, as if they were but matters for under-sheriffs and catch-poles; though many times those under-sheriffries do more good than their high speculations. St. Paul, when he boasts of himself, doth oft interlace, " I speak like a fool ; " but speaking of his calling, he saith, " Magnificabo apostolatum meum."

LIV

OF VAIN GLORY

It was prettily devised of Æsop, the fly sat upon the axle-tree of the chariot wheel, and said, " What a dust do I raise ! " So are there some vain persons, that, whatsoever goeth alone, or moveth upon greater means, if they have never so little hand in it, they think it is they that carry it. They that are glorious must needs be factious ; for all bravery stands upon comparisons. They must needs be violent to make good their own vaunts ; neither can they be secret, and therefore not effectual ; but, according to the French proverb, " *beaucoup de bruit, peu de fruit* "—much bruit, little fruit. Yet certainly, there is use of this quality in civil affairs : where there is an opinion and fame to be created, either of virtue or greatness, these men are good trumpeters. Again, as Titus Livius noteth, in the case of Antiochus and the Ætolians, there are sometimes great

effects of cross lies, as if a man negotiates between two princes, to draw them to join in a
war against a third, doth extol the forces of
either of them above measure, the one to the
other ; and sometimes he that deals between
man and man raiseth his own credit with both,
by pretending greater interest than he hath in
either ; and in these, and the like kinds, it
often falls out that somewhat is produced of
nothing ; for lies are sufficient to breed opinion,
and opinion brings on substance.

In military commanders and soldiers, vain
glory is an essential point ; for as iron sharpens
iron, so by glory one courage sharpeneth
another. In cases of great enterprise upon
charge and adventure, a composition of glorious
natures doth put life into business ; and those
that are of solid and sober natures have more
of the ballast than of the sail. In fame of
learning, the flight will be slow without some
feathers of ostentation : " Qui de contemnenda
gloria libros scribunt, nomen suum inscribunt."
Socrates, Aristotle, Galen, were men full of
ostentation : certainly vain glory helpeth to
perpetuate a man's memory ; and virtue was
never so beholden to human nature as it received its due at the second hand. Neither
had the fame of Cicero, Seneca, Plinius Secundus, borne her age so well if it had not been
joined with some vanity in themselves like unto

varnish, that makes ceilings not only shine, but last.

But all this while, when I speak of vain glory, I mean not of that property that Tacitus doth attribute to Mucianus, " Omnium, quæ dixerat feceratque, arte quadam ostentator : " for that proceeds not of vanity, but of natural magnanimity and discretion ; and in some persons it is not only comely, but gracious : for excusations, cessions, modesty itself, well governed, are but arts of ostentation ; and amongst those arts there is none better than that which Plinius Secundus speaketh of, which is, to be liberal of praise and commendation to others, in that wherein a man's self hath any perfection ; for, saith Pliny, very wittingly, " In commending another, you do yourself right ; " for he that you commend is either superior to you in that you commend, or inferior ; if he be inferior, if he be to be commended, you much more ; if he be superior, if he be not to be commended, you much less.

Vain glorious men are the scorn of wise men, the admiration of fools, the idols of parasites, and the slaves of their own vaunts.

LV

OF HONOUR AND REPUTATION

THE winning of honour is but the revealing of a man's virtue and worth without disadvantage ; for some in their actions do woo and affect honour and reputation—which sort of men are commonly much talked of, but inwardly little admired—and some contrariwise, darken their virtue in the show of it, so as they be undervalued in opinion. If a man perform that which hath not been attempted before, or attempted and given over, or hath been achieved, but not with so good circumstance, he shall purchase more honour than by effecting a matter of greater difficulty, or virtue, wherein he is but a follower. If a man so temper his actions, as in some one of them he doth content every faction or combination of people, the music will be the fuller. A man is an ill husband of his honour that entereth into any action, the failing wherein may disgrace him more than the carrying of it through can honour him. Honour that is gained and broken upon another hath the quickest reflection, like diamonds cut with fascets ; and, therefore, let a man contend to excel any competitors of his honour, in out-shooting them if he can, in their own bow. Discreet followers and servants help much to reputation: "Omnis fama a domesticis emanat." Envy, which is the canker of honour, is best extinguished by declaring a man's self in his ends, rather to seek merit than fame : and by attributing a man's successes rather to divine Providence and felicity than to his own virtue or policy. The true marshalling of the degrees of sovereign honour are these : in the first place are "conditores imperiorum," founder of States and commonwealths ; such as were Romulus, Cyrus, Cæsar, Ottoman, Ismael : in the second place are "legislatores," lawgivers ; which are also called second founders, or "perpetui principes," because they govern by their ordinances after they are gone : such were Lycurgus, Solon, Justinian, Edgar, Alphonsus of Castile, the wise, that made the "Siete partidas " : in third place are "liberatores," or "salvatores " ; such as compound the long miseries of civil wars, or deliver their countries from servitude of strangers or tyrants ; as Augustus Cæsar, Vespasianus, Aurelianus, Theodoricus, King Henry the Seventh of England, King Henry

the Fourth of France : in the fourth place are
" propagatores," or " propugnatores imperii,"
such as in honourable wars enlarge their terri-
tories, or make noble defence against invaders :
and in the last place, are " patres patriæ," which
reign justly, and make the times good wherein
they live ; both which last kinds need no
examples, they are in such number. Degrees
of honour in subjects are, first, " participes
curarum," those upon whom princes do discharge the greatest weight of their affairs ; their
right hands, as we may call them : the next
are " duces belli," great leaders ; such as are
princes' lieutenants, and do them notable services in the wars : the third are " gratiosi,"
favourites ; such as exceed not this scantling,
to be solace to the sovereign, and harmless to
the people : and the fourth, " negotiis pares " ;
such as have great places under princes, and
execute their places with sufficiency. There is
an honour, likewise, which may be ranked
amongst the greatest, which happeneth rarely ;
that is, of such as sacrifice themselves to death
or danger for the good of their country ; as
was M. Regulus, and the two Decii.

LVI

OF JUDICATURE

JUDGES ought to remember that their office is *jus dicere*, and not " jus dare "—to interpret law, and not to make law, or give law—else will it be like the authority claimed by the Church of Rome, which, under pretext of exposition of Scripture, doth not stick to add and alter, and to pronounce that which they do not find, and by show of antiquity to introduce novelty. Judges ought to be more learned than witty, more reverend than plausible, and more advised than confident. Above all things, integrity is their portion and proper virtue. " Cursed (saith the law) is he that removeth the landmark." The mislayer of a mere-stone is to blame ; but it is the unjust judge that is the capital remover of landmarks, when he defineth amiss of land and property. One foul sentence doth more hurt than many foul examples ; for these do but corrupt the stream, the other

must beware of hard constructions and strained
inferences ; for there is no worse torture than
the torture of laws ; especially in case of laws
penal, they ought to have care, that that which
was meant for terror be not turned into
rigour : and that they bring not upon people
that shower whereof the Scripture speaketh,
" Pluet super eos laqueos ; " for penal laws
pressed are a shower of snares upon the people :
therefore let penal laws, if they have been
sleepers of long, or if they be grown unfit for
the present time, be by wise judges confined
in the execution : " Judicis officium est, ita
tempora rerum," &c. In causes of life and
death, judges ought (as far as the law permitteth) in justice to remember mercy, and to
cast a severe eye upon the example, but a
merciful eye upon the person.

Secondly, for the advocates and counsel that
plead. Patience and gravity of hearing is an
essential part of justice, and an over-speaking
judge is no well-tuned cymbal. It is no grace
to a judge first to find that which he might
have heard in due time from the bar, or to
show quickness of conceit in cutting off evidence or counsel too short, or to prevent information by questions, though pertinent. The
parts of a judge in hearing are four :—to direct
the evidence ; to moderate length, repetition
or impertinency of speech ; to recapitulate

select, and collate the material po
which hath been said ; and to give
sentence. Whatsoever is above
much, and proceedeth either of
willingness to speak, or of impati
or of shortness of memory, or
stayed and equal attention. It
thing to see that the boldness
should prevail with judges, where
imitate God, in whose seat they
presseth the presumptuous, and g
the modest ; but it is more stran
should have noted favourites, wh
cause multiplication of fees an
by-ways. There is due from
the advocate some commendatio
where causes are well handled a
especially towards the side w
not, for that upholds in the cli
tion of his counsel, and beats d
conceit of his cause. There is
the public a civil reprehensio
where there appeareth cunnin
neglect, slight information, inc
or an over-bold defence. A
counsel at the bar chop with
wind himself into the handl
anew, after the judge hath
tence ; but, on the other side
meet the cause half-way, no

the
hear
T
mini
plac
the f
ough
corr
ture
thist
with
of ca
The
instru
sowe
and t
those
tion,
" para
her b
tages
accou
that a
shifts,
direct
obliqu
the po
the co
tice to
flies fo

corrupteth the fountain—so saith Solomon, " Fons turbatus, et vena corrupta est justus cadens in causa sua coram adversario."

The office of judges may have a reference unto the parties that sue, unto the advocates that plead, unto clerks and ministers of justice underneath them, and to the sovereign or State above them.

First, for the causes of parties that sue. There be (saith the Scripture) " that turn judgment into wormwood ; " and surely there be also that turn it into vinegar ; for injustice maketh it bitter, and delays make it sour. The principal duty of a judge is to suppress force and fraud, whereof force is the more pernicious when it is open, and fraud when it is close and disguised. Add thereto contentious suits, which ought to be spewed out as the surfeit of courts. A judge ought to prepare his way to a just sentence, as God useth to prepare his way by raising valleys and taking down hills ; so when there appeareth on either side a high hand, violent persecution, cunning advantages taken, combination, power, great counsel, then is the virtue of a judge seen to make inequality equal ; that he may plant his judgment as upon even ground. " Qui fortiter emungit, elicit sanguinem ; " and where the wine-press is hard wrought, it yields a harsh wine, that tastes of the grape-stone. Judges must beware of hard constructions and strained inferences ; for there is no worse torture than the torture of laws ; especially in case of laws penal, they ought to have care, that that which was meant for terror be not turned into rigour : and that they bring not upon people that shower whereof the Scripture speaketh, " Pluet super eos laqueos ; " for penal laws pressed are a shower of snares upon the people : therefore let penal laws, if they have been sleepers of long, or if they be grown unfit for the present time, be by wise judges confined in the execution : " Judicis officium est, ita tempora rerum," &c. In causes of life and death, judges ought (as far as the law permitteth) in justice to remember mercy, and to cast a severe eye upon the example, but a merciful eye upon the person.

Secondly, for the advocates and counsel that plead. Patience and gravity of hearing is an essential part of justice, and an over-speaking judge is no well-tuned cymbal. It is no grace to a judge first to find that which he might have heard in due time from the bar, or to show quickness of conceit in cutting off evidence or counsel too short, or to prevent information by questions, though pertinent. The parts of a judge in hearing are four :—to direct the evidence ; to moderate length, repetition or impertinency of speech ; to recapitulate, select, and collate the material points of that which hath been said ; and to give the rule or sentence. Whatsoever is above these is too much, and proceedeth either of glory and willingness to speak, or of impatience to hear, or of shortness of memory, or of want of a stayed and equal attention. It is a strange thing to see that the boldness of advocates should prevail with judges, whereas they should imitate God, in whose seat they sit, who represseth the presumptuous, and giveth grace to the modest ; but it is more strange that judges should have noted favourites, which cannot but cause multiplication of fees and suspicion of by-ways. There is due from the judge to the advocate some commendation and gracing, where causes are well handled and fair pleaded, especially towards the side which obtaineth not, for that upholds in the client the reputation of his counsel, and beats down in him the conceit of his cause. There is likewise due to the public a civil reprehension of advocates, where there appeareth cunning counsel, gross neglect, slight information, indiscreet pressing, or an over-bold defence. And let not the counsel at the bar chop with the judge, nor wind himself into the handling of the cause anew, after the judge hath declared his sentence ; but, on the other side, let not the judge meet the cause half-way, nor give occasion to the party to say his counsel or proofs were not heard.

Thirdly, for that that concerns clerks and ministers. The place of justice is a hallowed place ; and therefore not only the bench, but the footpace and precincts, and purprise thereof, ought to be preserved, without scandal and corruption ; for, certainly, grapes (as the Scripture saith) " will not be gathered of thorns or thistles ; " neither can justice yield her fruit with sweetness amongst the briars and brambles of catching and polling clerks and ministers. The attendance of courts is subject to four bad instruments : first, certain persons that are sowers of suits, which make the court swell, and the country pine : the second sort is of those that engage courts in quarrels of jurisdiction, and are not truly " amici curiæ," but " parasiti curiæ," in puffing a court up beyond her bounds for their own scraps and advantages : the third sort is of those that may be accounted the left hands of courts ; persons that are full of nimble and sinister tricks and shifts, whereby they pervert the plain and direct courses of courts, and bring justice into oblique lines and labyrinths : and the fourth is the poller and exacter of fees, which justifies the common resemblance of the courts of justice to the bush, whereunto while the sheep flies for defence in weather, he is sure to lose part of the fleece. On the other side, an ancient clerk, skilful in precedents, wary in proceedings, and understanding in the business of the court, is an excellent figure of a court, and doth many times point the way to the judge himself.

Fourthly, for that which may concern the sovereign and estate. Judges ought, above all, to remember the conclusion of the Roman twelve tables, " Salus populi suprema lex ; " and to know that laws, except they be in order to that end, are but things captious, and oracles not well inspired : therefore it is a happy thing in a State, when kings and states do often consult with judges : and again, when judges do often consult with the king and State : the one, where there is matter of law intervenient in business of State ; the other when there is some consideration of State intervenient in matter of law ; for many times the things deduced to judgment may be " meum " and " tuum," when the reason and consequence thereof may trench to point of estate : I call matter of estate, not only the parts of sovereignty, but whatsoever introduceth any great alteration or dangerous precedent : or concerneth manifestly any great portion of people ; and let no man weakly conceive that just laws, and true policy, have any antipathy ; for they are like the spirits and sinews, that one

moves with the other. Let judges also remember that Solomon's throne was supported
by lions on both sides : let them be lions, but
yet lions under the throne ; being circumspect,
that they do not check or oppose any points of
sovereignty. Let not judges also be so ignorant of their own right as to think there is not
left them, as a principal part of their office, a
wise use and application of laws ; for they may
remember what the apostle saith of a greater
law than theirs, " Nos scimus quia lex bona est,
modo quis ea utatur legitime."

LVII

OF ANGER

To seek to extinguish anger utterly is but a bravery of the Stoics. We have better oracles : " Be angry, but sin not : let not the sun go down upon your anger." Anger must be limited and confined, both in race and in time. We will first speak how the natural inclination and habit " to be angry " may be attempered and calmed ; secondly, how the particular motions of anger may be repressed, or, at least, refrained from doing mischief ; thirdly, how to raise anger, or appease anger in another.

For the first there is no other way but to meditate and ruminate well upon the effects of anger, how it troubles man's life ; and the best time to do this is to look back upon anger when the fit is thoroughly over. Seneca saith well " that anger is like ruin, which breaks itself upon that it falls." The Scripture ex-

horteth us " to possess our souls in patience ";
whosoever is out of patience, is out of possession of his soul.   Men must not turn bees :

" Animasque in vulnere ponunt."

Anger is certainly a kind of baseness, as it
appears well in the weakness of those subjects
in whom it reigns, children, women, old folks,
sick folks.   Old men must beware that they
carry their anger rather with scorn than with
fear, so that they may seem rather to be above
the injury than below it, which is a thing
easily done, if a man will give law to himself
in it.

For the second point, the causes and motives
of anger are chiefly three ; first, to be too
sensible of hurt, for no man is angry that feels
not himself hurt, and, therefore, tender and
delicate persons must needs be oft angry, they
have so many things to trouble them which
more robust natures have little sense of ; the
next is, the apprehension and construction of
the injury offered to be, in the circumstances
thereof, full of contempt—for contempt is that
which putteth an edge upon anger, as much,
or more, than the hurt itself ; and, therefore,
when men are ingenious in picking out circumstances of contempt, they do kindle their anger
much ; lastly, opinion of the touch of a man's

reputation doth multiply and sharpen anger, wherein the remedy is that a man should have, as Gonsalvo was wont to say, " telam honoris crassiorem." But in all refrainings of anger, it is the best remedy to win time, and to make a man's self believe that the opportunity of his revenge is not yet come ; but that he foresees a time for it, and so to still himself in the meantime, and reserve it.

To contain anger from mischief, though it take hold of a man, there be two things whereof you must have special caution : the one, of extreme bitterness of words, especially if they be aculeate and proper ; for " communia male-dicta " are nothing so much ; and again, that in anger a man reveal no secrets ; for that makes him not fit for society : the other, that you do not peremptorily break off in any business in a fit of anger : but howsoever you show bitterness, do not act anything that is not revocable.

For raising and appeasing anger in another, it is done chiefly by chusing of times when men are forwardest and worst disposed to incense them ; again, by gathering (as was touched before) all that you can find out to aggravate the contempt ; and the two remedies are by the contraries : the former to take good times, when first to relate to a man an angry business, for the first impression is much ; and the other is, to sever, as much as may be, the construction of the injury from the point of contempt ; imputing it to misunderstanding, fear, passion, or what you will.

LVIII

OF VICISSITUDES OF THINGS

SOLOMON saith, " There is no new thing upon the earth : " so that as Plato had an imagination that all knowledge was but remembrance, so Solomon giveth his sentence, " That all novelty is but oblivion ; " whereby you may see that the river of Lethe runneth as well above ground as below. There is an abstruse astrologer that saith, " If it were not for two things that are constant (the one is, that the fixed stars ever stand at like distance one from another, and never come nearer together, nor go farther asunder ; the other that the diurnal motion perpetually keepeth time), no individual would last one moment." Certain it is, that matter is in a perpetual flux, and never at a stay. The great winding-sheets that bury all things in oblivion are two, deluges and earthquakes. As for conflagrations and great droughts, they do not merely dispeople but destroy. Phaeton's car went but a day: and the three years' drought, in the time of Elias, was but particular, and left people alive. As for the great burnings by lightnings, which are often in the West Indies, they are but narrow; but in the other two destructions, by deluge and earthquake, it is farther to be noted that the remnant of people which hap to be reserved are commonly ignorant and mountainous people, that can give no account of the time past; so that the oblivion is all one, as if none had been left. If you consider well of the people of the West Indies, it is very probable that they are a newer or a younger people than the people of the old world; and it is much more likely that the destruction that hath heretofore been there was not by earthquakes (as the Egyptian priest told Solon, concerning the island of Atlantis, that it was swallowed by an earthquake), but rather that it was desolated by a particular deluge—for earthquakes are seldom in those parts: but on the other side, they have such pouring rivers, as the rivers of Asia, and Africa, and Europe are but brooks to them. Their Andes likewise, or mountains, are far higher than those with us; whereby it seems that the remnants of generations of men were in such a particular deluge saved. As for the observation that Machiavel hath, that the jealousy of sects doth much extinguish the memory of things—traducing Gregory the Great, that he did what in him lay to extinguish all heathen antiquities—I do not find that those zeals do any great effects, nor last long; as it appeared in the succession of Sabinian, who did revive the former antiquities.

The vicissitudes, or mutations, in the superior globe are no fit matter for this present argument. It may be, Plato's great year, if the world should last so long, would have some effect, not in renewing the state of like individuals (for that is the fume of those that conceive the celestial bodies have more accurate influences upon these things below than indeed they have), but in gross. Comets, out of question, have likewise power and effect over the gross and mass of things; but they are rather gazed upon, and waited upon in their journey, than wisely observed in their effects, especially in their respective effects; that is, what kind of comet, for magnitude, colour, version of the beams, placing in the region of heaven or lasting, produceth what kind of effects.

There is a toy, which I have heard, and I would not have it given over, but waited upon a little. They say it is observed in the Low Countries (I know not in what part), that every five and thirty years the same kind and

sute of years and weathers comes about again ;
as great frosts, great wet, great droughts, warm
winters, summers with little heat, and the like ;
and they call it the prime : it is a thing I do
the rather mention, because, computing back-
wards, I have found some concurrence.

But to leave these points of nature, and to
come to men. The greatest vicissitude of
things amongst men is the vicissitude of sects
and religions ; for these orbs rule in men's
minds most. The true religion is built upon
the rock ; the rest are tossed upon the waves
of time. To speak, therefore, of the causes of
new sects, and to give some counsel concerning
them, as far as the weakness of human judgment
can give stay to so great revolutions.

When the religion formerly received is rent
by discords, and when the holiness of the pro-
fessors of religion is decayed and full of scandal,
and withal the times be stupid, ignorant, and
barbarous, you may doubt the springing up of
a new sect ; then also there should arise any
extravagant and strange spirit to make himself
author thereof—all which points held when
Mahomet published his law. If a new sect
have not two properties, fear it not, for it will
not spread : the one is the supplanting, or the
opposing of authority established—for nothing
is more popular than that ; the other is the
giving licence to pleasures and a voluptuous life ;

for as for speculative heresies (such as were in ancient times the Arians, and now the Arminians), though they work mightily upon men's wits, they do not produce any great alteration in States, except it be by the help of civil occasions. There be three manner of plantations of new sects—by the power of signs and miracles; by the eloquence and wisdom of speech and persuasion; and by the sword. For martyrdoms, I reckon them amongst miracles, because they seem to exceed the strength of human nature: and I may do the like of superlative and admirable holiness of life. Surely there is no better way to stop the rising of new sects and schisms than to reform abuses; to compound the smaller differences, to proceed mildly, and not with sanguinary persecutions; and rather to take off the principal authors, by winning and advancing them, than to enrage them by violence and bitterness.

The changes and vicissitudes in wars are many, but chiefly in three things; in the seats or stages of the war, in the weapons, and in the manner of the conduct. Wars, in ancient time, seemed more to move from east to west; for the Persians, Assyrians, Arabians, Tartars (which were the invaders) were all eastern people. It is true the Gauls were western; but we read but of two incursions of theirs—the one to Gallo-Græcia, the other to Rome;

but east and west have no certain points of heaven, and no more have the wars, either from the east or west, any certainty of observation ; but north and south are fixed ; and it hath seldom or never been seen that the far southern people have invaded the northern, but contrariwise—whereby it is manifest that the northern track of the world is in nature the more martial region—be it in respect of the stars of that hemisphere, or of the great continents that are upon the north ; whereas the south part, for aught that is known, is almost all sea, or (which is most apparent) of the cold of the northern parts, which is that, which, without aid of discipline, doth make the bodies hardest, and the courage warmest.

Upon the breaking and shivering of a great State and empire, you may be sure to have wars ; for great empires, while they stand, do enervate and destroy the forces of the natives which they have subdued, resting upon their own protecting forces ; and then when they fail also, all goes to ruin, and they become a prey ; so it was in the decay of the Roman empire, and likewise in the empire of Almaigne, after Charles the Great, every bird taking a feather, and were not unlike to befall to Spain, if it should break. The great accessions and unions of kingdoms do likewise stir up wars ; for when a State grows to an over power, it is like a great flood, that will be sure to overflow, as it hath been seen in the States of Rome, Turkey, Spain, and others. Look when the world hath fewest barbarous people, but such as commonly will not marry, or generate, except they know means to live (as it is almost everywhere at this day, except Tartary), there is no danger of inundations of people ; but when there be great shoals of people, which go on to populate, without foreseeing means of life and sustentation, it is of necessity that once in an age or two they discharge a portion of their people upon other nations, which the ancient northern people were wont to do by lot—casting lots what part should stay at home, and what should seek their fortunes. When a warlike State grows soft and effeminate, they may be sure of a war ; for commonly such States are grown rich in the time of their degenerating, and so the prey inviteth, and their decay in valour encourageth a war.

As for the weapons, it hardly falleth under rule and observation ; yet we see even they have returns and vicissitudes ; for certain it is, that ordnance was known in the city of the Oxydraces in India, and was that which the Macedonians called thunder, and lightning, and magic, and it is well known that the use of ordnance hath been in China above two thousand years. The conditions of weapons and their improvements are, first, the fetching afar off, for that outruns the danger, as it is seen in ordnance and muskets ; secondly, the strength of the percussion, wherein likewise ordnance do exceed all arietations and ancient inventions ; the third is, the commodious use of them, as that they may serve in all weathers, that the carriage may be light and manageable, and the like.

For the conduct of the war : at the first men rested extremely upon number ; they did put the wars likewise upon main force and valour, pointing days for pitched fields, and so trying it out upon an even match, and they were more ignorant in ranging and arraying their battles. After, they grew to rest upon number rather competent than vast, they grew to advantages of place, cunning diversions, and the like, and they grew more skilful in the ordering of their battles.

In the youth of a State, arms do flourish, in the middle age of a State, learning, and then both of them together for a time ; in the declining age of a State, mechanical arts and merchandise. Learning hath his infancy, when it is but beginning, and almost childish ; then his youth, when it is luxuriant and juvenile ; then his strength of years, when it is solid and reduced ; and, lastly, his old age, when it waxeth dry and exhaust. But it is not good to look too long upon those turning wheels of vicissitude, lest we become giddy. As for the philology of them, that is but a circle of tales, and therefore not fit for this writing.

LIX

A FRAGMENT OF AN ESSAY ON FAME

THE poets make Fame a monster; they describe her in part finely and elegantly, and in part gravely and sententiously; they say, look how many feathers she hath, so many eyes she hath underneath, so many tongues, so many voices, she pricks up so many ears.

This is a flourish: there follow excellent parables; as that she gathereth strength in going; that she goeth upon the ground, and yet hideth her head in the clouds; that in the day-time she sitteth in a watch-tower, and flieth most by night; that she mingleth things done with things not done; and that she is a terror to great cities; but that which passeth all the rest is, they do recount that the earth, mother of the giants that made war against Jupiter, and were by him destroyed, thereupon in anger brought forth Fame; for certain it is that rebels, figured by the giants, and seditious fames and libels, are but brothers and sisters, masculine and feminine ; but now if a man can tame this monster, and bring her to feed at the hand, and govern her, and with her fly other ravening fowl and kill them, it is somewhat worth. But we are infected with the style of the poets. To speak now in a sad and serious manner, there is not in all the politics a place less handled, and more worthy to be handled, than this of fame ; we will therefore speak of these points ; what are false fames, and what are true fames, and how they may be best discerned, how fames may be sown and raised, how they may be spread and multiplied, and how they may be checked and laid dead, and other things concerning the nature of fame. Fame is of that force as there is scarcely any great action wherein it hath not a great part, especially in the war. Mucianus undid Vitellius by a fame that he scattered, that Vitellius had in purpose to move the legions of Syria into Germany, and the legions of Germany into Syria ; whereupon the legions of Syria were infinitely inflamed. Julius Cæsar took Pompey unprovided, and laid asleep his industry and preparations by a fame that he cunningly gave out, how Cæsar's own soldiers loved him not ; and being wearied of the wars, and laden with the spoils of Gaul, would forsake him as soon as he came into Italy. Livia settled all things for the succession of her son Tiberius, by continually giving out that her husband Augustus was upon recovery and amendment; and it is a usual thing with the bashaws to conceal the death of the Great Turk from the janizaries and men of war, to save the sacking of Constantinople, and other towns, as their manner is. Themistocles made Xerxes, King of Persia, post apace out of Grecia, by giving out that the Grecians had a purpose to break his bridge of ships which he had made athwart the Hellespont. There be a thousand suchlike examples, and the more they are, the less they need to be repeated, because a man meeteth with them everywhere; wherefore, let all wise governors have as great a watch and care over fames, as they have of the actions and designs themselves.

LX

THE PRAISE OF KNOWLEDGE

SILENCE were the best celebration of that which I mean to commend ; for who would not use silence, where silence is not made ? and what crier can make silence in such a noise and tumult of vain and popular opinions ? My praise shall be dedicated to the mind itself. The mind is the man, and the knowledge of the mind. A man is but what he knoweth. The mind itself is but an accident to knowledge, for knowledge is a double of that which is. The truth of being, and the truth of knowing, is all one ; and the pleasures of the affections greater than the pleasures of the senses. And are not the pleasures of the intellect greater than the pleasures of the affections ? Is it not a true and only natural pleasure, whereof there is no satiety ? Is it not knowledge that doth alone clear the mind of all perturbations ? How many things are there which we imagine not ! How many things do we esteem, and value otherwise than they are ! This ill-proportioned estimation, these vain imaginations, these be the clouds of error that turn into the storms of perturbation. Is there any such happiness as for a man's mind to be raised above the confusion of things, where he may have the prospect of the order of nature, and the error of men ? Is this but a vein only of delight, and not of discovery ?—of contentment, and not of benefit ? Shall we not as well discern the riches of nature's warehouse as the benefit of her shop ? Is truth ever barren ? Shall we not be able thereby to produce worthy effects, and to endow the life of man with infinite commodities ? But shall I make this garland to be put upon a wrong head ? Would anybody believe me if I should verify this, upon the knowledge that is now in use ? Are we the richer by one poor invention, by reason of all the learning that hath been these many hundred years ? The industry of artificers maketh some small improvement of things invented ; and chance sometimes, in experimenting, maketh us to stumble upon somewhat which is new ; but all the disputation of the learned never brought to light one effect of nature before unknown. When things are known and found out, then they can descant upon them, they can knit them into certain causes, they can reduce them to their principles. If any instance of experience stand against them, they can range it in order by some distinctions. But all this is but a web of the wit; it can work nothing. I do not doubt but that common notions, which we call reason, and the knitting of them together, which we call logic, are the art of reason and studies. But they rather cast obscurity than gain light to the contemplation of nature.

All the philosophy of nature which is now received is either the philosophy of the Grecians, or that of the alchemists. That of the Grecians hath the foundations in words, in ostentation, in confutation, in sects, in schools, in disputations. The Grecians were, as one of themselves saith, *you Grecians, ever children*. They knew little antiquity; they knew, except fables, not much above five hundred years before themselves. They knew but a small portion of the world. That of the alchemists hath the foundation in imposture, in auricular traditions and obscurity. It was catching hold of religion, but the principle of it is, *Populus vult decipi*. So that I know no great difference between these great philosophers, but that the one is a loud crying folly, and the other is a whispering folly. The one is gathered out of a few vulgar observations, and the other out of a few experiments of a furnace. The one never faileth to multiply words, and the other ever faileth to multiply gold. Who would not smile at Aristotle when he admireth the eternity and invariableness of the heavens, as there were not the like in the bowels of the earth? Those be the confines and borders of these two kingdoms, where the continual alteration and incursion are. The superficies and upper parts of the earth are full of varieties. The superficies and lower parts of the heavens, which we call the middle region of the air, are full of variety. There is much spirit in the one part that cannot be brought into mass. There is much massy body in the other place that cannot be refined to spirit. The common air is as the waste ground between the borders. Who would not smile at the astronomers, I mean not these new carmen which drive the earth about, but the ancient astronomers, which feign the moon to be the swiftest of the planets in motion, and the rest in order, the higher the slower; and so are compelled to imagine a double motion; whereas how evident is it, that that which they call a contrary motion is but an abatement of motion? The fixed stars overgo Saturn, and so in them and the rest all is but one motion, and the nearer the earth the slower—a motion also whereof air and water do participate, though much interrupted.

But why do I in a conference of pleasure enter into these great matters, in sort that pretending to know much, I should forget what is seasonable? Pardon me, it was because all things may be endowed and adorned with speeches, but knowledge itself is more beautiful than any apparel of words that can be put upon it. And let not me seem arrogant without respect to these great reputed authors. Let me so give every man his due, as I give Time his due, which is to discover truth. Many of these men had greater wits, far above mine own, and so are many in the universities of Europe at this day. But, alas! they learn nothing there but to believe; first, to believe that others know that which they know not; and after, themselves know that which they know not. But, indeed, facility to believe, impatience to doubt, temerity to answer, glory to know, doubt to contradict, end to gain, sloth to search, seeking things in words, resting in part of nature; these, and the like, have been the things which have forbidden the happy match between the mind of man and the nature of things, and in place thereof have married it to vain notions and blind experiments; and what the posterity and issue of so honourable a match may be, it is not hard to consider.

Printing, a gross invention; artillery, a thing that lay not far out of the way; the needle, a thing partly known before: what a change have these three made in the world in these times; the one in state of learning, the other in state of the war, the third in the state of treasure, commodities, and navigation! And those, I say, were but stumbled upon and lighted upon by chance. Therefore, no doubt, the sovereignty of man lieth hid in knowledge; wherein many things are reserved, which kings with their treasure cannot buy, nor with their force command; their spials and intelligencers can give no news of them, their seamen and discoverers cannot sail where they grow. Now we govern nature in opinions, but we are thrall unto her in necessities; but if we would be led by her in invention, we should command her in action.

THE END

Printed in Great Britain by
Thomas Nelson and Sons Ltd, Edinburgh